THE BOOK OF JOB
Mankind on Trial

THE BOOK OF JOB
MANKIND ON TRIAL

A modern interpretation
of the most perplexing problem of all ages.
Suffering seems to be
an inalienable heritage of the human race.
The Book of Job asks "Why suffering?"
This Book supplies five answers.

by

Rabbi Joshua S. Sperka, B.A., M.A.

BLOCH PUBLISHING CO.
New York, New York 10010

Library of Congress Catalog No. 79-51154
ISBN: 0-8197-0470-9

Printed in U.S.A. by Harlo Printing Company, Detroit, Michigan

This Book is Dedicated
to the Memory and Martyrdom
of the Six Million Jews
murdered by the Nazi Barbarians.
This crime was
resisted by few, assisted by many,
with the indifferent silence of the
entire civilized world.

Table of Contents

Preface

The closing sentence in the Book of the prophet Hosea has been my guiding light in the preparation of this book. "Whoever is wise, let him understand these things; Whoever is discerning let him know them; that the ways of the Lord are right and the righteous walk in them, while the sinners stumble in them." There are various ways to interpret the Book of Job. My method has been exclusively traditional.

My distinguished scholarly colleague and friend, Rabbi Dr. David S. Shapiro, Professor at the University of Wisconsin, wrote to me after reading this manuscript. Here is his observation.

> "Your commentary will undoubtedly make for interesting reading for its insight into the text as well as for the many enlightening passages and quotations from the Talmud and Midrash, which you cite to confirm your interpretation, as well as the delightful parables with which you sprinkle your comments."

Years of teaching, toil and study inspired me to translate the complex Book of Job. It took years to compose the commentary of this complicated Book of the Bible.

For easier reading, I have translated the book from the original Hebrew. To facilitate understanding I have arranged the book into logical units and divisions, with an introductory note before each unit. I then presented the newly translated text, followed by my commentary.

I am grateful and thankful to the Almighty for granting me the opportunity to elucidate and comment on this holy book as a means of strengthening our faith and sanctifying His Name.

There are three books in the Bible that constitute its wisdom literature. In 1969 I translated and published the Book of Proverbs, and in 1973 the Book of Ecclesiastes. This, the Book of Job, is the third in the series of the wisdom Books.

I want to acknowledge the enormous contributions made to this book by my daughter Judith (Mrs. Matthew Clark), who helped in editing and made suggestions of structure and composition.

A note of thanks to my learned son Shlomo, who despite a very busy career, took time to review and make valuable suggestions in text and composition.

My profound thanks to my wife Yetta who, seeing the importance of the book, encouraged me and assisted me in every way in reviewing, composing, typing and editing.

To Dr. Samuel Stollman of Windsor, Ontario, my thanks for his review of the first part of this book.

Tradition ordains reverence for the sacred name of the Almighty. You will, therefore, find name of the Diety not fully spelled out in this book.

10

Introduction

The reason for suffering has been a perplexing question in all ages. The Book of Job critically explores this problem and therefore is most pertinent to our age. The popular explanation of suffering and evil in the world is challenged by Job. The concept that suffering comes as punishment for wickedness conflicts with the reality of life. What, then, is the answer to the problem of human suffering?

Just as the subject of the book is remarkable, so is its treatment. Instead of presenting this question as an abstract philosophical problem, the Book deals with the specific practical case of one man, Job. Because the Book is person-oriented, it has a special appeal to the reader. The Book mirrors a basic aspect of people's lives. Job complains: "Why do I suffer without cause or knowing the reason why?"

The Book's appeal contains a message because many people feel that they suffer without knowing the reason for their pain. People seeking a reason for their suffering or for evil in the world will greatly benefit by a study of Job.

The Book of Job, consisting of forty two chapters, can logically be divided into five parts.

Part one, the prologue, introduces Job and his family. It describes his position of great wealth and high honor which is transformed into misfortune and grave suffering. Part two contains the dialogue between Job and his friends. Part three introduces a new young voice, that of Elihu. Part four brings the book to a climax with the revelation of G-d from the whirlwind. Part five concludes the book with an epilogue in prose.

In Job, the reader will learn five answers to the question raised by this book. The prologue gives one definite answer; Job is not being punished for any sin whatsoever. Job's suffering is a test of his faith.

The dialogue contains three cycles of speeches of Job's three friends who present the conventional theology that suffering is the consequence of sin.

Job cries out in protest that his suffering is without cause since he believes himself without sin.

Elihu suggests that suffering is a form of education and purification. G-d imposes suffering only after warning and admonition fail.

G-d's answer from the whirlwind refutes any possible human comprehension of transcendental divine purposes. But G-d's answer does more than respond to the question of evil in the world. It indicates to humanity the place of man in the universe. G-d repeats once again his call to Adam. "Where are you, man," "What are you, man, doing to avoid evil in the world?"

I am incensed at the flippancy of many writers on the Book of Job whose interpretation puts G-d on trial. That is the reason for the title of this book: Job—Mankind on Trial.

The revelations of G-d in the whirlwind describe G-d's role in the creation of the world. It is man's task, as I develop my thesis in this book, to become a partner in creating a better world and ultimately hastening the messianic era.

THE BOOK OF JOB
Mankind on Trial

PART I

PROLOGUE

Introductory Note

first two chapters of the Book of Job contain a
prologue. The hero of the Book is introduced as
was a man in the Land of Uz whose name was Job."
resented as a man of complete integrity. He was
with great wealth, honor and a large family.
the scene shifts to heaven. In response to G-d's
about this good man, Job, Satan cynically questions
ety. "Just take away his possessions," says Satan to
d he will curse you to your face."
is so certain of Job's piety that He permits the test
faith. Job experiences total ruin, but he withstands
His possessions are robbed and burned. His children
Job does not rebel against G-d. On the contrary,
s, "The Lord has given and the Lord has taken
lessed be the name of the Lord."
cond test is given to Job. Satan minimizes the first
st try to touch his person, his bones and his flesh,"
tan, and Job will blaspheme G-d.
now is smitten with a loathsome physical illness.
counsels him to curse G-d and die. Job admonishes

his wife saying, "Shall we accept the good from G-d and not accept the evil?"

The prologue ends with Job's three friends, Eliphaz, Bildad, and Zophar coming to comfort him. Disheartened by the tragedy and misery of Job, they perform rites of mourning, tearing part of their garments and sitting in silence for seven days.

Chapter 1

VERSES 1 THROUGH 5

TEXT

There was a man in the Land of Uz whose name was Job and that man was blameless and upright and one who feared G-d and avoided evil. There were born to him seven sons and three daughters. He possessed seven thousand sheep, three thousand camels, five hundred teams of oxen, five hundred female donkeys and he had very many servants and he was the greatest of all the men of the East. His sons used to hold a feast in the house of each one, on his day in turn, and they invited their three sisters to eat and drink with them. And when the day of their feasting was over, Job would send for them and bless them and he would rise up early in the morning and offered burnt offerings according to the number of them all. For Job thought: 'Perhaps my children have sinned and blasphemed G-d in their hearts,' and this Job had always done.

COMMENTARY

The Book of Job begins with the words "There was a man in the Land of Uz whose name was Job and that man was blameless," etc. To begin the Book with the words "There was a man" instead of beginning with the name of the person who is the subject of the book (as "The vision of Isaiah," "The words of Jeremiah," "The words of Amos," "The vision of Obadiah") emphasizes the fact that the author has done this purposely. He wants to direct the reader not so much to the name Job, but rather to the word, "man," implying that the story he will tell is applicable to "man," to every man.

The Book of Job portrays the struggle of a troubled soul. It depicts the inner agony which all must face who experience grief, disaster, and sorrow. Job reflects the conflict that rages in the soul of a suffering man who asks, why is there evil and suffering in the world? The Book seeks to answer this question.

Chapter 1

VERSES 6 THROUGH 12

TEXT

Now there was the day when the angels came to stand in the presence of the Lord and Satan also came among them. And the Lord said to Satan: "Where did you come from?" and Satan answered, "From going back and forth on the earth and walking up and down on it." And the Lord said to Satan: "Have you considered my servant Job that there is none like him on earth; a man blameless and upright who fears G-d and avoids evil." Then Satan answered the Lord: Is it for nothing that Job fears G-d. Have you not protected him and his house and all that he owns on every side; you have blessed the works of his hands and his possessions increased in the land. But just put out Your hand now and touch whatever he owns and he will curse You to Your face." And the Lord said to Satan: "Here, all he has is in your power, only upon himself do not lay your hands." So Satan went out from the presence of the Lord.

COMMENTARY

Job does not know of the plot to test him. Suddenly he will suffer deprivation and disease. Job like every man in

21

distress, will voice the cry, "Why did this happen to me?"

In most cases this remains one of the unanswered questions in life. The Book of Job teaches us that the reason for suffering is hidden from man. In this book the author places the plotting of Job's suffering in heaven. The conversation between G-d and Satan is not revealed. One must conclude then, that the reason for suffering is hidden from man on earth.

There is a very comforting thought that can be drawn from the reading of this Book. Here Job suffers not for punishment of sin, but as a test of his faith. The Midrash sees this as a lesson why so often the pious suffer. When it comes to a test, one does not select the weak, but the strong. Rabbi Jonathan said: "A potter does not test weak vessels because he cannot give them a single blow without breaking them. Similarly, the Holy One blessed be He, does not test the wicked, but only the righteous."

Can there be benefit from pain? The story is told about a man in distress who came to see his Rabbi. The visitor culminated the outpouring of his fate by saying, "My condition is very bad." Instead of hearing words of comfort, the troubled man was shocked to hear his Rabbi reply, "One must not say my fate is bad, one should say it is bitter, it is not bad. It is in fact, good." The Rabbi continued, "Most people take the bitter medicine of experience and, unfortunately, it is not only bitter, but it is also bad. In their failure to derive a lesson from their experience they lose the healing power it can bring."

Chapter 1

VERSES 13 THROUGH 22

TEXT

And there was a day when his sons and his daughters were eating and drinking wine in their oldest brother's house. A messenger came to Job saying: "The oxen were plowing and the donkeys feeding beside them. And the Sabeans attacked and seized them, they have slain the servants with the edge of the sword, and I alone have escaped to tell you." While he was still speaking another came and said: "Lightning fell from heaven and has burned up the sheep and servants and consumed them, and I alone have escaped to tell you." While he was still speaking another came and said: "Your sons and your daughters were eating and drinking wine in their oldest brother's house. And a mighty wind swept in from the desert and struck the four corners of the house and it fell upon the young people and they are dead, and I alone have escaped to tell you." Then Job rose and tore his robe and shaved his head and fell down upon the ground and worshipped. He said: "Naked I came from my mother's womb and naked I shall return; the Lord gave and the Lord has taken away, blessed be the name of the Lord." In all this, Job did not sin or blame G-d.

COMMENTARY

In this section of the book the author indicates a superb, extraordinary reaction to the loss of loved ones. The usual aching void felt after a loss is all negative. The pain of the loss is so deep that we cannot think of the positive aspect of having been enriched by that life.

Job says at the loss of his children, "The Lord has given, the Lord has taken, praised be the name of the Lord." Job, in his hour of anguish, does not first think, "The Lord has taken." He begins by saying, "The Lord has given," then he says, "The Lord has taken back." Job implies that sadder than losing a loved one is never having had one to lose.

The Talmudic story of Bruria, the wife of Rabbi Meir, exemplifies this reaction to a great loss (Midrash, Proverbs 31). The two sons of this couple died on a Sabbath. When Rabbi Meir came home from the synagogue at the end of the Sabbath, his wife asked Rabbi Meir a question of law. "Someone left two jewels with us some time ago. He came to claim them. Should I return them to the owner?" The Rabbi replied, "Of course you must return the jewels." She then took her husband by the arm and led him into the room where their sons were. On seeing them dead he started to cry, "My sons, my sons." Then Bruria reminded him tearfully, "You said we must return our two jewels to the owner who had entrusted them to our care. The Lord has given, the Lord has taken back His very own."

Chapter 2

VERSES 1 THROUGH 6

TEXT

And there was a day, when the angels came to stand in the presence of the Lord and Satan also came to stand before the Lord. And the Lord said to Satan: "Where have you come from?" And Satan replied to the Lord: "From going back and forth on the earth and walking up and down on it." And the Lord said to Satan: "Have you considered my servant Job that there is none like him on the earth, a man blameless and upright who fears G-d and avoids evil; he still holds fast to his integrity, though you incited me against him to harm him without cause." Satan replied to the Lord: "Skin for skin, a man will give all that he has to save his life. But just reach out your hand and touch his bone and flesh and he will curse you to your face." And the Lord said to Satan: "He is in your hand, only spare his life."

COMMENTARY

In the above scene in heaven G-d permits the testing of Job's faith through physical suffering. The question often asked by commentators and readers carries with it a reproach to G-d for the apparently arbitrary concession to Satan that Job be tested through suffering. It is asked: "Just because Satan does not believe the testimony that Job is 'blameless and upright who fears G-d and avoids evil' should Job be tested through suffering?"

My interpretation leads us to a positive lesson in this trial. It involves not Job as an individual but deals with the subject of the survival of mankind. The true question here is, "Was the creation of man a mistake?" Many are the Midrashic sources relating that, at the time of the world's creation, the angels actively opposed the creation of man. Satan in this book may well be seen following this antagonistic approach towards man.

As we find in the Zohar on Job: "And there was a day when the angels came to stand in the presence of the Lord and Satan also came among them to stand before the Lord." (1:6) The Zohar comments: "It is written that the angels stood before G-d but it is not recorded what they said." The intent is that they came to stand against the original Divine decision to create man. They said then: "What is man that Thou knowest him?" "Why did You create man?" (Leket Shmuel-Zohar)

This must be read with a puzzling comment linking Job with Noah, found in the Midrash: "If Job came only to explain to us the episode of the generation of the flood, it would have been sufficient." (Midrash Rabbah, Gen. 26)

There is, of course, no direct reference to Noah in the Book of Job. Rather these two Midrashim indicate that the testing of Job was an attempt to prove that the experiment of the creation of man was not a total failure since at least one good man could be found. Job and Noah stand in similar relationship to their contemporaries.

During the generation of the flood, mankind was so corrupt that even G-d admitted the failure of man. As we find in Genesis 6:5-7: "When the Lord saw that the wickedness of man on earth was great and that the whole trend of his thinking was only towards evil, the Lord regretted that He had made man on earth and He was grieved to the heart. And the Lord said, 'I will blot out the man whom I have created from the face of the earth.' "

G-d was prepared to destroy His creation. However, one good man, Noah, was found. "But Noah found favor in the eyes of the Lord." (Gen. 6:8) He was saved and with him the future of man on earth. This episode is repeated in the days of Job. Rabbi Yochanan said: "The generation of Job was addicted to lewdness." (Talmud Baba Bathra 15b)

Job then is not tested because Satan doubts G-d's testimony of Job's integrity. Job reflects a repetition of the episode of Noah.

Job is tested to prove once again that the experiment of the creation of man has not been a total failure. One truly good man justified the experiment of the creation of man, and answered the objections of the angels. Rabbi Chiya, son of Abba, said in the manner of Rabbi Yochanan: "Even for the sake of one righteous man does the world endure, as it is said: (Proverbs 10:25) 'But the righteous is the foundation of the world.' " (Yoma 38b)

"The matter can be compared to the case of a king who had an orchard planted with one row of fig trees, one of vines, one of pomegranates, and one of apples. He entrusted it to a tenant and went away. After a time the king came and looked in at the orchard to ascertain what it had yielded. He found it full of thorns and briars, so he brought woodcutters to raze it. He looked closely at the thorns and noticed among them a single rose colored flower. He smelled it and his spirits calmed down. The king said: 'The whole orchard shall be saved because of this flower.' " (Midrash Rabbah Leviticus 23:3)

It is even more significant that Job's withstanding his test shows that there is the potential in every man to attain perfect faith. The divine purpose is the perfecting of man to attain the messianic age.

Chapter 2

VERSES 7 THROUGH 10

TEXT

So Satan went out from the presence of the Lord and afflicted Job with sore boils from head to foot. And he took a piece of broken pottery to scrape himself as he sat among the ashes. Then his wife said to him, "Do you still hold fast to your piety? Curse G-d and die." And he said to her: "You speak as one of the impious women would speak; shall we accept good from G-d and not accept evil?" Even in all this, Job did not sin with his lips.

COMMENTARY

Job's reaction to his affliction is expressed to his wife: "Shall we accept the good from G-d and not accept the evil?" In the following Talmudic story, a Talmudic sage chooses to accept a fate of suffering. Rabbi Eliezer ben P'doss was very poor. Once, when he had nothing to eat, he took a skin of garlic and put it into his mouth. The Rabbis who came to visit him noticed that he was crying and laughing in his sleep. When he awoke they asked him, "Why did you cry and laugh?" He replied that Divine Providence was sitting by his side. He said, "I asked, 'How long will I suffer in this world?' And the answer came, 'Eliezer, my son, would you rather I remake the world? Perhaps you might be born at a happier hour.' I said, 'All this, and then only perhaps?' I then asked, 'Which is the greater portion of my life, the part that I have already lived, or the part that I am still to live?' The reply was, 'The part that you have already lived.' Then I said, 'If so, I do not want it.' " (Talmud Taanith 25)

Job says: "Shall we accept the good from G-d and not accept the evil?" In this Talmudic story, Rabbi Eliezer, who had so little of the good life, accepts his suffering. Rabbi Zushia, we shall find, attained the saintly attitude that even suffering must be for the good. All his life he suffered afflictions and failing health, but he never complained. Because of his deep faith, he accepted his misery and misfortune as his fate. But he never questioned G-d's ways.

We find in the Chassidic book *Matzmiach Yeshu'os* that Rabbi Shmelke of Nicholsberg and his brother asked the beloved teacher, the "Maggid of Mezerich," "Why do the righteous suffer?" His answer: "Go and see the saintly Rabbi Zushia of Hanipol. He can answer your question." They traveled to Hanipol and asked the Rabbi: "What is the meaning of suffering?"

Rabbi Zushia smiled and told them; "This question you ask me? I don't know. Suffering and pain have never been my lot in life. G-d has ever given me the good and I bless His name for it. *For whatever G-d gives me must be for the good."* Rabbi Zushia, the saint, believed that even suffering had its place and purpose.

Chapter 2

VERSES 11 THROUGH 13

TEXT

Then Job's three friends heard of the calamity which had befallen him, they came each from his own home, Eliphaz the Temanite, and Bildad the Shuhite, and Zophar the Namathite, for they arranged to go together and to comfort him. When they saw him in the distance they could not recognize him, they raised their voices and wept; and they each tore his robe, and they cast dust over their heads towards heaven. Then they sat with him on the ground seven days and seven nights and none said a word to him for they saw that his agony was very great.

COMMENTARY

The author relates the coming of Job's three friends as they heard of Job's distress and the reaction it brought upon them.

In Genesis the Bible portrays the meeting of Joseph and Benjamin as follows: "And he (Joseph) fell upon his brother Benjamin's neck and wept and Benjamin wept upon his neck." (Genesis 45:14) Rashi quotes the Midrash (also in Talmud Megilla 16b): "Joseph wept for the Temple which was to be in Benjamin's territory and would ultimately be destroyed and Benjamin wept for the Tabernacle which was to be in Joseph's territory and would ultimately be destroyed." This raises a question: Why did not Joseph and Benjamin each weep and lament the destruction of the sanctuary in his own territory? Why did they weep for the destruction of the sanctuary in the other's territory? The answer given by a Chassidic Rabbi is that they had attained such a level of love for each other that each one subdued his own pain and lamented the suffering of the other. Love of another must be so deep that the trouble of his friend is more painful than one's own.

Parables and Anecdotes

ON THE BOOK OF JOB
"Moses wrote the Book of Job" (Baba Bathra 14b), to console the children of Israel in the midst of their slavery in Egypt. "You say that Moses wrote his book (the Book of Moses), the section of Balaam and Job. This supports the opinion of Rabbi Joshua who said that Job was a contemporary of Moses."

—Baba Bathra 15a

"A certain Rabbi was sitting before Rabbi Samuel ben Nachmani and in the course of his exposition remarked that 'Job never was and never existed, but is only a parable.' " Rabbi Samuel replied, "To refute people such as you, the text says, 'There was a man in the Land of Uz, Job was his name.' (Job 1:1) But the Rabbi answered, 'If that is so, what of the verse 'The poor man had nothing, but one small ewe lamb, which he had bought and nourished.' (II Samuel 12:3, parable of prophet to King David.) Was that anything but a parable? So this, too is a parable.' 'If so,' said Rabbi Samuel, 'why are his name and the name of the town mentioned?' "

—Baba Bathra 15a

31

"He (Job) existed, but he did not experience suffering. So why are they—suffering and agony—mentioned in the book? To teach us that if the suffering would have come upon him, he would have withstood them."

—Yerushalmi, Sotah 5:6

JOB

"Let your house be opened wide. How so? This teaches that a man's house should have a spacious entrance on the north, south, east and west, like Job's who made four doors to his house. And why did Job make four doors to his house? So that the poor would not be troubled to go all around the house. One coming from the north could enter straight, one coming from the south could enter straight, and so from all directions. For that reason Job made four doors to his house."

—Avoth D'reb Nathan 7:1

"On that day Rabbi Joshua ben Hyrcanas expounded: Job only served G-d from love, as it is said 'Though He slay me, yet will I trust in Him' (Job 13:15). And should it be still doubtful whether the meaning is 'I will trust in Him' or 'I will not trust' (Variant in text, written 'No' loh with aleph; read 'to Him' loh with vav), there is another text to declare 'Until I die I will not put away my integrity from me.' (Job 27:5) This teaches us that what he did was from love. Rabbi Joshua said: 'Who will remove the dust from your eyes, Rabbi Yochanan ben Zackai, since you have been expounding all your life that Job only served G-d from fear, as it is said, 'That man was perfect and upright, and one who feared G-d and avoided evil.' (Job 1:1) Did not Joshua, the pupil of your pupil, teach that what he (Job) did was from love?' "

—Mishna Sotah 27b

"Rabbi Chiya ben Abba said in the name of Rabbi Simoi: There were three in that plan (to destroy Israel

32

through the decree 'Every son that is born ye shall cast in the river.' Exodus 1:22), Balaam, Job, and Yisro. Balaam, who devised it, was slain. Job, who quietly acquiesced, was afflicted with sufferings. Yisro, who fled, merited that his descendents would sit in the Chamber of Hewn Stone."— (where the Sanhedrin met)

—Sotah 11a

ON MAN

"It is taught:" Rabbi Meir said, 'The first man (to be created) was gathered from all parts of the earth."

—Sanhedrin 38a

"The creatures of heaven were created in His image and His likeness and do not reproduce. The animals of earth reproduce but were not created in His image and His likeness. Then G-d said, 'I will create him (man) in My image and likeness like the creatures of heaven, and he will reproduce like the creatures of the earth.' G-d said, 'If I will create man only as a creature of heaven, he will live and never die. If I create man only as a creature of earth, he will die and not live. Therefore I shall create him as both of heaven and earth. If he will live, he will die, and if he dies he will live.' "

—Yalkut Shimoni 1:14

"Man was created alone (only one man). Why so? That the heretics might not say that there are many ruling powers in heaven. Another answer: For the sake of the righteous and the wicked. That the righteous might not say: Ours is a righteous heredity (we have no need to avoid temptation). The wicked might not say: Ours is an evil heredity (we have no power to resist temptation). Another answer: For the sake of the families, that they may not quarrel with each other (about the superiority of their respective ancestry). Now, even though only one was created they quarrel, how much more if two had been created?

Another answer: Because of robbers and plunderers. Though one was originally created, people rob and plunder. How much more, had two been created. (Each claiming that the land originally belonged to his first ancestor.)

—Sanhedrin 38a

"Rabbi Simon said: When the Holy One, blessed be He, came to create Adam, the ministering angels divided into many groups and factions. Some said: 'Let him be created.' Some said: 'Let him not be created.' Mercy said: 'Let him be created, for he will do good deeds.' Truth said: 'Let him not be created, for he will be full of falsehood.' Righteousness said: 'Let him be created, for he will perform righteous acts. Peace said: 'Let him not be created for he will be full of strife.'

"Rabbi Huna said: While the angels were discussing and disputing, the Holy One, Blessed be He, created man. Then He said to them: 'What are you arguing about? Man is already made.' "

—Midrash Rabba Genesis 8:5

JUDGING THE WORLD

"Now there was the day when the angels came to stand in the presence of the Lord and Satan also came among them." (Job 1:6) The day was Rosh Hashana (New Year) on which day human creatures pass before G-d in judgment. The defending angels defend and the accusing angels prosecute, and Satan comes to prosecute."

—Mayon Ganim, Job 1:6

"Rabbi Yossi says: 'Man is judged every day,' as it says, 'And you visit him every morning.' (Job 7:18) Rabbi Nathan says: 'Man is judged every moment,' as it says, 'You try him every moment.' (Job 7:18)

—Rosh Hashana 16a

34

"Rabbi Eliezer then expounded on the verse: 'And there was a day when the angels came to stand before the Lord and Satan came among them.' (Job 1:6) This 'day' he said was Rosh Hashana (New Year) on which G-d sits in judgement on the world . . . The truth is, however, that on Rosh Hashana two sides stand before G-d for the judgement of mankind. The men of whom good deeds and repentence can be recorded are privileged to be inscribed for life and whoever is on this side is inscribed for life. But those whose deeds are evil, are assigned to the other side, which is death. Sometimes, however, it happens that the world is as it were exactly balanced between the two. Then if there is but one righteous person to tip the scale the world is saved. But if one wicked over balances, then the world is condemned to death. And in such a condition were the affairs of men in the time of Job. Then Satan stood before the Lord eager to denounce the world. Immediately, G-d asked Satan, 'Have you considered my servant Job? And as Satan heard this name he concentrated all his attention upon him.'

—Zohar 'Bo'

TEST

"As Rabbi Acha said: 'G-d created the 'Yetzer Hora' (evil inclination) only to test human beings.' "

—Zohar, Vayero

"With ten temptations was Abraham our father tempted and he stood steadfast in all of them, to show how great was the love of Abraham our father." (toward G-d)

—Avoth 5:3

"He (Satan) said before Him, 'Sovereign of the Universe, I have traversed the whole world and found none so faithful as your servant Abraham. For you did say to him, 'Arise, walk through the land, to the length and the breadth of it, for to you I will give it.' (Genesis 13:17) And even so, when he was unable to find any place in which to bury

35

Sarah until he bought one for four hundred shekels of silver, he did not complain against your ways.' "

—Baba Bathra 15b

"Happy the man who can withstand the test for there is none whom G-d does not prove. He tests the rich man, to see if his hand will be open to the poor and the poor man, He tries, in order to see whether he will accept chastisement without anger. As it says, 'And that you bring the poor that are humbled to your house.' (Isaiah 58:7) If the rich man withstands his test and practices charity, then he will enjoy his wealth in this world while the capital (reward for his good deeds) will be preserved for him in the world to come. And G-d will redeem him from the punishment of 'Gehinom' as it says, 'Happy is he who considers the poor; the Lord will deliver him in the day of evil.' (Psalm XLI:2) If the poor man withstands his test without rebelling, he receives a double portion in the world to come, as it says, 'For you save the afflicted people.' (Psalm XVIII:28) From where can you learn this? From Job, who suffered in this world and whom G-d repaid in double measure, as it says, 'And the Lord gave Job twice as much as he had before.'

—Midrash Rabba Mishpatim 31

SATAN

A Tana taught: "He (Satan) comes down to earth and misleads, then ascends to heaven and arouses wrath." (asks permission to take away a soul).

—Baba Bathra 16a

"Resh Lokish said, 'Satan, Yetzer (evil inclination), and the Angel of Death are all one.' "

—Baba Bathra 16a

"Rabbi Isaac said: 'Satan's torment was worse than that of Job. For this may be compared to a servant who is told by his Master, "Break the cask, but do not let any of the wine spill." ' "

—Baba Bathra 16a

"The (Hebrew) letters of 'Ha-Satan' (The Satan) have the numerical value of three hundred and sixty-four, indicating that on three hundred and sixty-four days of the year he has power to oppose, but on the Day of Atonement he does not have that power."

—Yoma 20a

EVIL INCLINATION
"G-d created two inclinations, one good, the other evil."

—Brochoth 61a

"Rabbi Assi stated 'The evil inclination is at first like the thread of a spider, but ultimately (if his temptations are permitted) he becomes as strong as cart ropes.' "

—Brochoth 52b

"Rabba observed: 'First he (evil inclination) is called a passer-by, then he is called a guest, and finally he is called a man.' "

—Brochoth 52b

"They (the people) said: 'Since this is a time of grace, let us pray that lust be eliminated. They prayed for mercy, and Satan was handed over to them. He (the prophet) said to them: "Realize that if you kill him, the world will come to an end." They imprisoned him for three days. They sought a fresh egg in the whole Land of Israel, and could not find it.' "

—Yoma 69b

"And G-d saw that everything He had made, behold it was very good." (Genesis (1:31) Rabbi Nachman said in the name of Rabbi Samuel, "Behold it was very good," that is the evil impulse. But is the evil impulse "very good?" That is astonishing. Yet, were it not for the evil impulse, men would not build homes, take wives, or propagate, or engage in business. And Solomon said the same: "I considered all labor and excelling in work, that is a man's rivalry with his neighbor." (Ecclesiastes 4:4)

—Midrash Rabba Genesis 11:9

REACTION TO SUFFERING

"It is incumbent on man to bless (G-d) for the evil, in the same way as for the good, as it says: 'And you should love the Lord your G-d with all your heart, with all your soul, and all your might.' (Deuteronomy 6:5) 'With all your heart' means your two impulses, the evil impulse as well as the good impulse. 'With all your soul' means even though he takes your soul. 'With all your might' means with all your money. Another explanation of 'with all your might' is, whatever treatment he metes out to you."

—Mishna Brochoth 54

"When Rabbi Akiva was taken out for execution it was the hour for the recital of the 'Shema' and while they combed his flesh with iron combs, he was accepting upon himself the Kingship of Heaven (saying the 'Shema'). His disciples said to him, 'Our teacher, even to this point?' He answered, 'All my days I have been troubled by this verse "with all your soul" (which I expounded) even if He takes your soul. I said, 'When shall I have the opportunity of fulfilling this? Now that I have the opportunity, shall I not fulfill it?' He prolonged the word Echad (one) until he expired while saying it.' "

—Brochoth 61b

FRIENDS OF JOB

"Then Job's three friends heard of the calamity that had befallen him. They came each from his own home, Eliphaz the Tamanite, Bildad the Shuhite, and Zophar the Naama-thite, for they arranged to go together to mourn with him and to comfort him." (Job 2:11) What is the meaning of "they arranged to go together?"

"Rabbi Judah said in the name of Rav: 'It teaches that they all entered through one gate, although it has been taught each lived three hundred parsongs away from the other. How did they know (of Job's troubles)? Some say they had crowns (each crown had a portrait of a friend. In case of trouble, the portrait changed) and some say that they had certain trees, the withering of the tree was a sign to them. Rova said: This bears out the popular saying: Either a friend like the friends of Job, or death."

—Baba Bathra 16b

PART II

DIALOGUE

Introductory Note

The poetic dialogue between Job and his friends com·prises the bulk of the book.

Job begins with an outburst of grief and lament. He is provoked to anger by the accusations of his friends who say his suffering must be punishment for his sins. He refutes them, insisting on his innocence. The severity of his suffering and the harshness of his friends bring him to a stage of confusion. He repeatedly declares his innocence, and that punishment such as his is undeserved.

In his agony, Job generalizes his personal suffering, claiming that universally the just are punished and the wicked prosper. His faith in G-d never falters but he is seeking an answer from G-d. He begs for an indictment for his sins or a vindication for his plight.

The friends maintain one doctrine: G-d is just. He could only punish for sins. If Job suffers, he has sinned.

Job undergoes a spiritual experience as he develops his response to his friends. From utter bewilderment, he reaches a realization that in spite of all that has befallen him, G-d is witness to his innocence. He will ultimately vindicate him. "Though He slay me, I will trust in Him," and "As for me, I know my Redeemer lives."

This comprehension calms Job and he begins to assert his faith in G-d. Job realizes that there is a difference between human knowledge and Divine knowledge.

Job concludes with a description (Chapter 29) of his former grandeur. In Chapter 30 he narrates his present misery. In Chapter 31 he outlines the Biblical code of ethics he has lived by, to prove his innocence.

Chapter 3

TEXT

Afterward Job opened his mouth and cursed his day. And Job spoke and said: Let the day perish wherein I was born and the night which said 'a man-child is conceived.' Let that day be darkness; let not G-d regard it from above, neither let the light shine upon it. Let darkness and the shadow of death reclaim it, let a cloud dwell upon it, let all that make black the day, terrify it. As for that night, may deep darkness capture it, let it not be counted in the days of the year, nor enter in the number of the months. Lo, let that night be desolate and no sound of joy enter it. May they curse it who curse the day, who are prepared to rouse the leviathan. May the stars of its dawn be dark, may it hope for light but have none, nor see the eyelids of the morning. Because it did not close the doors of my mother's womb nor hid trouble from my eyes. Why did I not die in the womb or perish as I came forth from it? Why did the knees receive me? or why the breasts that I should suck? For now I should have lain down and been quiet; I should have slept, then were I at rest. With kings and counselors of the earth, who rebuild ruined places for themselves. Or with princes who have gold, who fill their houses with silver. Or as a hidden untimely birth, I should not be, as infants that never saw light. There, the wicked cease from troubling and there, the weary are at rest. All the prisoners are at ease, they hear not the voice of the taskmaster. There, the small and great are alike and the slave is free from his master. Why is light given to the wretched and life to the bitter in soul, who long for death, but it comes not and dig for it more than for buried treasures? Who would exult in joy and be happy if they could find a grave, for a man whose way is hidden, whom G-d had fenced in? For my sighing comes in place of my food and my groans are poured out like water. For the fear I had has come upon me, and what I was afraid of, befalls me. I was not at ease nor was I quiet, neither had I rest, but trouble came.

COMMENTARY

After seven days of silence, intense suffering and shock, Job gives angry, lamenting expression to his misery and tragedy.

In this chapter, Job does not seek a reason for his troubles. He does not protest the Divine judgment. He curses the day he was born and wishes he had never been born. He yearns for the peace and serenity that the dead experience, for the pain and agony is too much for him to bear.

Rabbi Yannai said: "It is not in our power to explain either the prosperity of the wicked or the afflictions of the righteous." (Mishna Avoth 4:19)

The reader, with a little objectivity, must realize that even if we never know the reason for suffering, suffering is part of the reality of life. No one escapes suffering, and perhaps it has its place and must have some unknown reason.

Pain may be a moral discipline. We can learn the unknown from the known. In medical science pain is seen as

46

a danger signal. Sometimes alarming and frightening, but nevertheless it comes as a warning that often shields life from destruction. Pain can reveal a disease which otherwise may go undiscovered until it is past remedy.

Historically we may detect that human pain and misery forced mankind to devise a measure of relief from pain and misery. Man's struggle also drove him to discover inventions. Even as tribulations and suffering hastened the growth of science, they brought healing and comfort to mankind.

Were it possible to remove all suffering it would not necessarily be an improvement of life. Every human being is subject to risks, hazards and many forms of physical and mental illness. Suppose a drug might be discovered that could render a normal human being immune to any and all biological and mental sickness, but at the price inducing within him a state of permanent euphoria. He would become a happy, but inactive and dull creature. This would not be an improvement over his original state. There is a saying: "Better a philosopher dissatisfied, than a fool satisfied."

We can lessen the severity of suffering if we find meaning and purpose in life. For one must try to reach one's goals even through suffering. There are instances of people whose suffering was accompanied by the discovery of a goal or a creative attitude, a meaning for life. Then the suffering is not only diminished, but can bring a person to a higher spiritual level, and a greater sense of fulfillment.

Ludwig von Beethoven suffered an increasing deafness from a disease of his youth. Yet he became one of the world's great composers and musicians. Helen Keller, deaf and blind from infancy, became a great author and lecturer. Franklin Roosevelt attained power and position in spite of his crippling disease.

Eliphaz in his opening address says: "Behold, happy is the man whom G-d corrects; therefore despise not the chastising of the Almighty" (Job 5:17). Elihu later in the book declares: "He (G-d) delivers the afflicted by affliction" (Job 36:15).

The Rabbis in the Talmud equate suffering with discipline. They speak of the entire episode of the Israelites' slavery in Egypt, their hunger and hardship while wandering in the desert, as part of G-d's fatherly discipline in order to make them a better people.

Painful experience that makes an individual better or that ultimately makes the world better, gives meaning to suffering that suffering is a pathway to improve life, is asserted in this Talmudical comment.

"G-d gave Israel three precious gifts and all of these were given only through suffering. These are: The Torah, the Land of Israel and the world to come. How do we know about Torah? Because it is written, 'Happy is the man whom you chastise, O Lord, and teach him out of your law' (Psalm 94:12). How do we know about the Land of Israel? Because it is said, 'As a man disciplines his son, so the Lord G-d has been disciplining you' (Deuteronomy 8:5). How do we know about the world to come? As it is written, 'For the commandment is a lamp and the teaching is light and the admonitions of discipline are the way of life' " Proverbs :23).

These three gifts are equally applicable to each individual person. "Torah" as the acquisition of learning, both spiritual and cultural, is not given without effort and sacrifice. "The Land of Israel," symbolic of roots and identity, is not offered to the individual without labor, exertion and work. "The world to come," the future for the individual, is not provided to him without hardship and discipline.

The following story illustrates the Biblical phrase "for even as a father disciplines his son, so the Lord your G-d has been disciplining you" (Deuteronomy 8:5).

A rich man had an only son. In order to encourage his studies and to train him to cope with competition, the father invited into his home an orphan boy. The boy would live together with his son. He would become his companion at study and at play. Unfortunately the orphan guest did not make the grade. He did not like to study. He was quarrelsome, and misbehaved. The foster father found that his attempt failed, so he asked the guest to leave the house. Some time later the father regretfully discovered that his own son neglected his studies, acted arrogantly and misbehaved. The father, seeing that admonition and words failed to correct him, set out to punish him and deprived him of many privileges.

The son complained to his father, "Why do you pour out all anger on me, your own son? I remember the orphan boy. He was no better than I. In a very calm manner you asked him to leave the house. That was all. With me you act angrily and you constantly punish me."

"Let me answer you," the father replied, "the orphan boy was a stranger in our home. As long as he was obedient, willing to learn and behaved, he was welcome. When he did not live up to my expectation, I had to send him away. That was all. But with you it is different. You are my son. My concern is to train and teach you and prepare you for your future. If I send you away from home, I would defeat my purpose. It is my duty to admonish and punish you, to make you change your ways. I have a responsibility to rear and raise you so that you take your place in our society. It is my duty and obligation to develop your capacities and your potentialities. Therefore I must correct you. My demands for your improvement and development may be painful to both of us. But the discipline and chastisement is for your own good. It is because I care about you and love you, that I do this to you. I am your father and it is my hope to see you grow up a good man."

Chapter 4

TEXT

Then Eliphaz the Temanite answered and said: If one tried a word with you, will you be weary? But who could refrain from speaking? Behold you have instructed many and strengthened weak hands. Your words have upheld the fallen and you have strengthened the feeble knees. But now that it comes to you, you are weary that it touches you, and you are troubled. Is not your fear of G-d, your confidence and your hope, the integrity of your ways? Remember, what innocent man ever perished? And where were the upright cut off? As I have observed, those who plough iniquity and sow trouble, reap it. By the breath of G-d they perish and by the blast of His wrath they are consumed. The lion roars and the fierce lion howls, and the teeth of the young lions are broken. The old lion perishes for lack of prey and the cubs of the lioness are scattered. Now a message was secretly brought to me and a whisper of it reached my ear. In thoughts from the visions of the night, when deep sleep falls on men, fear came upon me and trembling that all my limbs were frightened. A spirit passed before my face that made the hair of my flesh

*stand up. It stood still, but I could not discern its ap-
pearance, a form was before my eyes, in the silence I heard
a voice. "Can mortal man be just before G-d, can a man
be pure before his Maker? Even in His servants He puts no
trust; and His angels He charges with folly. How much
more those who dwell in houses of clay whose foundation
is in the dust, who are crushed before the moth. Between
morning and evening they are crushed; without anyone
regarding it, they perish forever. Is not their tent cord
plucked up within them? They die and that without
wisdom."*

Chapter 5

TEXT

'Call now, who is there to answer you? And to which of the holy ones will you turn? For anger kills the fool and envy slays the simpleton. I have observed the fool striking root, but suddenly I declared his dwelling cursed. His children are far from safety, and are crushed in the Judgment Gate with none to deliver them. Whose harvest the hungry will devour; and take it even from the thorns and the famished, swallow up their wealth. For affliction does not come from the dust, nor does trouble sprout from the earth. For man gives birth to trouble, as the sparks fly upward. But as for me I would seek G-d, to G-d I would commit my cause. Who does things, great and inscrutable wonders without number? Who gives rain on the earth and sends water upon the open places? He sets the lowly on high and lifts the mourners to salvation. Who frustrates the plans of the crafty so that their hands cannot achieve success? He catches the wise in their own craftiness and the counsel of the perverse comes to a quick end. In daytime they encounter darkness and at noon they grope as in the night. But He saves from the sword, their mouth and

the needy from the hand of the mighty. So the poor have hope and iniquity shuts its mouth. Behold, happy is the man whom G-d reproves, do not despise the chastisement of the Almighty. For He makes sore but binds up; He wounds but His hands bring healing. From six disasters He will save you, and in seven no evil will touch you. In hunger He will redeem you from death, and in war from the power of the sword. You shall be hid from the roaming slander; nor need you fear destruction when it comes. At destruction and famine you will laugh; nor should you be afraid of the beasts of the earth. For you will have a pact with the stones of the field; and be at peace with the beasts of the field. You will know that your tent is at peace; and when you visit your homestead you will miss nothing. You will know your children are many, and your offspring like the grass of the earth. You will come to your grave in ripe old age as a shock of grain comes up in its season. Behold, this we have searched out, so it is; hear it and know it for yourself.

COMMENTARY

The Book of Job seeks an answer to the question, "Why suffering?" Job at first speaks about his own undeserved suffering. As the debate progresses the larger question arises as to why suffering and evil is allowed by a G-d of justice and mercy.

Eliphaz and later Bildad and Zophar have one answer. They believe in divine retributive justice. Therefore all suffering is punishment for sin.

It is true that reward and punishment is a cardinal principle in religion. Yet the Talmud is critical of Job's friends. "If one is visited by suffering afflicted with disease, or loss of children, you must not speak to him as his companions spoke to Job." (Talmud, Baba Metziah 58b)

At the end of our book, G-d asks Job to pray on behalf of his friends. "The Lord said to Eliphaz, 'My anger is kindled against you and against your friends for you have not spoken of Me the things that are right as has My servant Job; and My servant Job shall pray for you.'" (42:7-8). How did Eliphaz, Bildad and Zophar misrepresent and misinterpret true religion? They were the defenders of G-d's total and immediate justice in contrast to Job's cry of apparent injustice in the divine rule.

It may be that they spoke only of the divine quality of justice. G-d is just. If Job suffers, therefore, he has sinned. They argued that G-d punishes sinners and rewards the upright at all times. Job, on the other hand, insists that some upright do suffer and some evildoers prosper.

The question arises, why were the defenders of retributive justice wrong and Job right? They were wrong because they spoke of absolute divine justice leaving no room for the divine quality of mercy and compassion.

One of the thirteen Divine Attributes is that G-d is long suffering. The Bible reveals that "The Lord, the Lord, a G-d full of compassion, gracious and slow to anger" (Exodus 34:6).

The Psalmist's prayer reads: "Gracious and merciful is the Lord, slow to anger and of great kindness" (145:8).

The concept that G-d is long-suffering is proclaimed in the Bible, recited in our prayers and remains G-d's promise to man. In the "Nielah" (closing Prayer) on Yom Kippur we repeat the prophecy of Ezekiel. "Have I any pleasure at all that the wicked should die, says the Lord G-d; and not rather that he should return from his ways and live" (Ezekiel 18:23).

"When Moses ascended on high, he found the Holy One, Blessed be He, sitting and writing 'long-suffering!' Said he to Him: 'Sovereign of the Universe, long-suffering to the righteous?' G-d replied 'Even to the wicked.' Moses said: 'Let the wicked perish.' G-d replied: 'You will see that you will need this in the future.'" (Talmud Sanhedrin 111a)

Another example of G-d's patience. When G-d made a covenant with Abraham the Bible tells us: "And the Lord said to Abraham, know indeed, that your seed will be a stranger in a land that is not theirs, and they will enslave them 400 years; and in the fourth generation they shall come here again; for the iniquity of the Amorite is not full." (Genesis 15:13,16)

Rashi comments: "After they go into exile in Egypt they will be there three generations and the fourth will return to this land. For the iniquity of the Amorite is not yet full enough that he should be driven out of his land until that time. For the Holy One, blessed be He, does not exact punishment from any nation until its measure is full, as it is said (Isaiah: 27:8) 'In her full measure will you contend with her when you send her away.' "

Divine patience with man, the good and the wicked, is our concept of a merciful G-d. But in the interim, while G-d is waiting for the wicked to repent, the wicked pursue their wickedness and their violence brings suffering to the world. Thus G-d's patience results in much suffering of innocent man.

It may be a bit ironic and paradoxical that G-d's attribute of mercy may prolong the rule of the wicked and indirectly cause evil and suffering on earth. The reason may be found in this; that if man and the world are to exist, G-d cannot punish them immediately. In the very beginning of creation, this option was presented to G-d. "If You want strict justice there can be no world, if You want a world you cannot have strict justice." Then G-d's love and mercy causes Him to wait for the wicked to repent. If mankind is not to perish because of this application of G-d's love for the world and His compassion for man, we must accept the inevitable suffering. That may be part of the mystery of seeing the prosperity of the wicked and the suffering of the righteous.

The friends of Job, failing to include compassion as a divine attribute, presented to Job an unrealistic picture of life which neither pleased G-d nor consoled Job.

Chapters 6 and 7

TEXT: CHAPTER 6

Then Job replied and said: Oh, that my anguish was indeed weighed and my calamity placed in the scales. For now it would be heavier than the sound of the sea, therefore my words are rash. For the arrows of the Almighty are in me and my spirit drinks their poison, the terrors of G-d are arrayed against me. Does the wild ass bray when he has grass? or the ox low over his fodder? Can tasteless food be eaten without salt? or is there any taste in the juice of mallows? My soul refuses to touch them; they are like uncleanliness in my food. Oh, that my request might be granted, and that G-d might reward my hope. Even that it would please G-d to crush me, to loose his hand and cut me off. Then I should still have the consolation as I would revel in unsparing pain that I never have denied the words of the Holy One. What is my strength that I should wait and what my end that I should be patient? Is my strength the strength of stones or is my flesh bronze? Is it that I have no help in me and sound wisdom has been driven from me? To the despairing should come mercy from his friend—by reason of fear of the Almighty—when he is forsaken. My brothers have been as treacherous as a desert stream, as streams that overflow their banks. They are black with ice, upon them the snow dissolves. But in the time of heat they vanish, when it is hot they dry up from their place. The paths of their way do wind, they go up into the waste and are lost. The caravans of Tema looked, the travellers of Sheba had hoped for them. They are disappointed because they trusted. When they come there, they are put to shame. Now you have become like him (the stream); you see a terror and you are afraid. Have I said: give to me? or from your wealth offer a bribe for me? Deliver me from the hand of an enemy or ransom me from the hand of oppressors? Teach me and I shall be silent. Make me understand where I have erred. How forceful are honest words, but what does your arguing prove? You think to reprove me with words, but count words of despair as wind. You would cast lots even for an orphan and dig a pit for your friend. Now, be pleased to look me in the face, I would surely not lie to your face. Turn back, please, let there be no wrong, turn back for my cause is just. Is there any wrong on my tongue? Or is my palate insensible to wrongdoing?

TEXT: CHAPTER 7

Is not service man's lot on earth, whose days are like those of a hireling? Like a slave who longs for the shade and like a hireling who hopes for his wages. So I have been alotted months of emptiness and nights of misery appointed to me. When I lie down I say: "when shall I arise? but the night is long and I am full of tossing until dawn. My flesh is clothed with worms and clods of dust; my skin hardens and breaks. My days are swifter than a weaver's shuttle, and they end without hope. Remember that my life is a breath, my eye will never again see good. The eye of him who sees me shall look on me no more while your eyes are upon me, I am gone." As a cloud dissolves and it is gone, so he who goes down to the grave does not come up. He will not return again to his house; nor will his place know him again. Therefore I will not restrain my mouth; I will speak out in the agony of my spirit, I will complain in the bitterness of my soul. Am I a sea, or a sea monster that You set a watch over me? When I say my bed shall comfort me, my couch ease my complaint. Then You frighten me with dreams and terrify me with visions, so that my soul chooses strangling death, rather than my bones. I loathe it, I shall not live forever, let me alone, for my days are but a breath. What is man that You should magnify him and give Your attention to him; and You remember him every morning and test him every moment? How long will You not look away from me nor let me alone till I swallow my saliva? If I have sinned what have I done to You, O watcher of man? Why have You made me Your target and I have become a burden to myself. Why don't You pardon my sin and remove my transgression? For now I shall lie down in the dust and when You will seek me and I shall not be.

COMMENTARY: CHAPTERS 6 AND 7

At the end of Chapter Seven, Job emphasizes his perplexing situation. He seeks a reason for his suffering, with the question, "What is man, that you should magnify him and give your attention to him; and you remember him every morning and test him every moment? . . . If I have sinned what have I done to You O Watcher of man?"

This question is not answered by his friends. They could have calmed Job by stressing more responsibility towards G-d because of man's unique position in life. G-d watches and tests man because man is the only known creature who has free will. "Privileged is man, for he was created in His image. But it was an act of special favor that it was made known to him that he was created in the image of G-d." (Mishna Avoth 3:18)

The first part, that man was created in the image of G-d, implies man's potential and the second that he was made aware of his potentialities. It is not enough to have a diamond. It is important to know and be aware of the quality and value of the diamond.

It is important in the scheme of life for man to know

that he possesses qualities. Man is the only known creature who can speak, think, and determine his actions. Hence he can become a saint or sinner. Man has freedom of choice. Therefore he has personal responsibility for the good or the evil he does. In the scheme of creation, man was created not as a puppet, but rather in the image and likeness of G-d.

In a sense, angels in heaven and animals on earth form two extremes. Angels have responsibility and no freedom of choice. Animals have freedom and no responsibility. Man has both freedom and responsibility. The mystics speak of man as half angel and half animal, created in divine precision of both equal parts. Man is privileged to express and choose good or evil. If he permits his good inclination (angelic part) to dominate, he is good. If he allows his evil inclinations (animalistic part) to rule, he is wicked. His freedom to choose often results in evil. Suffering then, is the unavoidable result of his evil acts. The possibility of sinning, even as his doing good, exists, because man has free will.

If suffering is a result of sin, and sin is the result of man's choice, would not the world be a happier place if all men were good? That is precisely the goal of humanity, that all men become good. It is only when there is a possibility to do evil, that doing good is a virtue.

The question is asked, why G-d did not create man uniformly good? If that were the case, man would be good not because he wants to be good, but would be automatically so. This would deprive man of his greatest glory, his free will and the ability to choose between good and evil. Since man is free to choose his acts, he must abide by moral guidelines.

The doctrine of free will imposes upon every human being a personal responsibility for his acts. Depriving man of his personal responsibility for his actions is a threat to civilization. For, if man is not bound by a moral code, he can become barbaric and brutal.

Philosophers have speculated on this subject negatively. They say: "If G-d is omniscient, He knows before hand what I will do. How can I have free will? I must do that and I no longer have any choice to do differently."

The Rabbis in the Mishna stated: "All is foreseen and power of choice is given" (Avoth 3:19). It is still up to each man to choose. In the Bible we find this declaration: "I have set before you life and death, the blessing and the curse, therefore choose life" (Deuteronomy 30:19). This forms the basis for our doctrine of free will.

That G-d's knowledge of man's action does not intrude on man's free will can be seen in this example. Suppose a mother warns her child not to touch the red hot stove. It is known and forseen by the mother that anyone touching this hot stove will burn his hand. This knowledge on the mother's part does not force the child to touch the stove. The child still has the choice of touching or not touching the stove. It is true, however, that there is the built-in consequence of suffering in the event the command is disobeyed.

Chapter 8

TEXT

Then Bildad the Shuhite answered and said: How long will you make such utterance since the words of your mouth are as a mighty wind? Does G-d pervert justice, does G-d pervert the right? If your sons have sinned against Him, He delivered them into the hands of their transgression. If you will seek G-d and make supplication to the Almighty, if you are pure and upright, He will watch over you and your righteous dwelling will be in peace. Though your beginning may be small, your end shall be very great. For inquire, I beg you, of the former generation and heed what their fathers searched out. For we are but of yesterday and know nothing because our days on earth are as a shadow. Will they not teach you and inform you and out of their understanding utter these words? Will papyrus grow where there is no marsh, will reeds flourish without water? While still green and uncut, it withers before any other herb. Such is the fate of all who forget G-d, and the hope of the G-dless perishes. His confidence is mere gossamer thread, his trust is but a spider's web. He leans upon his house, but it will not stand; he seizes hold of it but it will not endure.

His (plant) is fresh before the sun and its roots spread over his garden. Over a heap his roots are entwined as they penetrate the place of stones. If it is destroyed from its place it will deny him (saying) "I have not seen you." So this is the joy of His way and from the earth another springs. Surely G-d will not despise the perfect nor will He uphold the evildoers. He will yet fill your mouth with laughter and your lips with shouts of joy. Your enemies will be clothed with shame and the tent of the wicked shall be no more.

COMMENTARY

Bildad is so convinced of his belief in absolute retribution, that he uses a very painful argument. He alone mentions the death of Job's children, "If your children sinned against Him, He delivered them into the hands of their transgression."

What makes him so certain of his doctrines is that he bases his speech on the historic experience of the forefathers and the authority of the wisdom of the past. To clinch his argument, he cites the fact of the brevity of human life.

"For we are but of yesterday and know nothing because our days upon earth are as a shadow."

Bildad uses the premise of the shortness of human life as reason to accept the teaching of retribution. Bildad failed as a friend. He should have used the same premise to say that human life is too short to see divine justice work out its plan. More comforting to Job would have been the thought that the human span of life is too short to judge the eternal and universal order. It is true that mortal man is part of an immortal creation. It is equally true that no part can fairly judge the whole. It would take an omniscient to judge the omniscient.

Bildad says: "Our days upon earth are as a shadow." The Psalmist also uses a similar expression. The Rabbis ask: "As a shadow of what? If life is like a shadow of a wall there is essence in it. If life is like a shadow cast by a date palm there is essence in it. The Psalm of David comes and explains, "His days are as a shadow that passes away" (Psalm 144). Rabbi Huna said in the name of Rabbi Acha "Life is like a bird which flies past and its shadow passed with it." (Midrash Rabba Ecclesiastes 1:2)

The brevity and frailty of human life leads us to this conclusion. Job, who believes and seeks G-d, could have found some logic in the idea that no mortal finite human creature can judge his immortal infinite Divine Creator.

Shimon ben Zemach Duron relates a relevant episode on this subject. In a discussion between a king and his philosophic friend the latter said: "I am thinking that in comparison with the highest sphere, our planet earth is no more than a swampy region in a great sea. For even the earth is not totally inhabited, only little more than a quarter is inhabited. Even in the inhabited portion you will find that the northern part is uninhabited. And then, even in the inhabited portion, there are mountains and hills, deserts, forests and wilderness. How comparatively small is the inhabited part of the earth. I am in one of the innumerable cities. In that very city there are shops, streets and marketplaces. I am in one spot only. I am no more than a fragment of the place in which I dwell. If so small is my portion in this world, and this whole world is a little part of the universal plan of the Creator, how can I comprehend His presence and His mysteries."

Chapters 9 and 10

TEXT: CHAPTER 9

Then Job answered and said: To be sure, I know that it is so; how can a man be just before G-d? If one should desire to contend with Him one could not answer Him once in a thousand times. He is wise in heart, and mighty in strength; who has hardened himself against Him and prospered? He removes mountains and they know it not, overturning them in His anger. He shakes the earth from its place and its pillars tremble. He commands the sun and it does not rise, and seals up the stars. He alone stretches out the heavens and treads on the high waves of the sea. He has made the Bear and Orion, the Pleiades and the Constellations of the south. He does great things past finding out and wonder without number. Lo, He goes by me and I do not see Him, He passes on, but I do not perceive Him. Behold, He snatches away, who can hinder Him, who can say to Him "what are you doing?" G-d will not restrain His anger; Rahab's helpers stooped under Him. How much less could I answer Him and choose my words with Him? For even if I am right I would not **answer, I would have to beg mercy from my opponent. If**

I called Him and He had answered me, I cannot believe that He would hear my voice. He racks me with a tempest and increases my wounds without cause. He does not let me catch my breath but fills me with bitterness. If it be a matter of power, here He is, and if it be a matter of judgment who will summon me? Though I be right my mouth would condemn me, though I am blameless it would prove me perverse. I am blameless, I regard not myself, I despise my life. Therefore I say it is all one; He destroys the blameless and the wicked. If a calamity brings sudden death He mocks at the distress of the innocent. The earth is given into the hand of the wicked, He covers the faces of its judges; if not He, who then is it? My days are swifter than a runner, they speed away they see no good. They passed like sailing boats, like a vulture swooping upon prey. If I say I will forget my complaint, I will change my appearance and be cheerful. I fear all my pains, I know You will not set me free. I shall be condemned, so why should I labor in vain? If I should wash myself with snow and clean my hands with lye, yet You would plunge me into the pit and my clothes would abhor me. For He is not a man like me that I should answer Him; that we should come together in litigation. There is no arbiter between us who would lay his hand upon both of us. Let Him remove His rod from me and let not His fear terrify me. Then I would speak and not fear Him, for I am not so with myself. . . . .

TEXT: CHAPTER 10

My soul is weary of my life, I will give free expression to my complaint, I will speak in the bitterness of my soul. I will say unto G-d, "Do not condemn me, let me know why You quarrel with me. Is it good for You to oppress, to despise the work of Your hands and shine upon the counsel of the wicked? Have You eyes of flesh or do You see as a man sees? Are Your days as the days of a mortal or Your years like the years of a man? That You seek my iniquity and search for my sin. Though You know that I am not wicked and none can deliver from Your hand. Your hands fashioned me and made me together round about, yet You destroy me. Remember, I beseech You, You made me as clay and will return me to the dust. Have You not poured me out and curdled me like cheese? You have clothed me with skin and flesh, and knitted me together wih bones and sinews. You have granted me life and kindness and Your providence preserved my spirit. Yet these things You hid in Your heart, I know that this was with You. If I sin You watch me and will not absolve me from my guilt. If I be wicked, woe unto me and if I be righteous, I cannot raise my head, being filled with shame and see my affliction. If it exalts itself, You hunt me like a lion and again show wonder against me. You renew Your witnesses against me and You increase Your anger with me, host after host are against me. Why did You take me out of the womb? Would that I had expired and no eye had seen me. I should have been as though I had never been and had been carried from the womb to the grave. Are not my days few? cease then; turn away from me so that I may have a little respite. Before I go, never to return, to a land of darkness and the shadow of death. A land of utter darkness, as darkness the shadow of death without order, where the light is as darkness."

COMMENTARY: CHAPTERS 9 and 10

These two chapters contain what seem very heretical expressions by Job. "He destroys the innocent and the wicked" (9:22). "The earth is given into the hand of the wicked" (9:24). Yet Job is a man of deep faith. He never doubts or denies the existence of the infinite might of the Creator. It is in the midst of his misery and affliction, feeling that he is innocent of any sin, that Job makes these sweeping grievances.

Job, in spite of his total faith, cries out in his agony. He bemoans the misfortune and misery of his dreadful life. Jeremiah and Daniel also expressed in their anguish, rebellious thoughts about G-d's attributes.

The Talmud tells that Jeremiah and Daniel were overwhelmed by the destruction and distress of their people. Under these conditions the Rabbis justify their refusal to express the accepted form of divine attributes in their prayers. In the following excerpt of the Talmud, we learn why Jeremiah and Daniel omitted certain divine attributes and why the men of the Great Synod restored them.

Rabbi Joshua ben Levi said: "Why were they called men of the Great Synod? Because they restored the crown of the divine attributes to its ancient completeness. (For) Moses had come and said: 'The great G-d, the mighty and the awful.' Then Jeremiah came and said: 'Aliens are destroying His Temple. Where are, then, His awful deeds?' Hence he omitted (the attribute) the 'awful.' Daniel came and said: 'Aliens are enslaving His sons. Where are His mighty deeds? Hence he omitted the word 'mighty.' But they came and said: 'On the contrary! Therein lie His mighty deeds in that He suppresses His wrath, that He extends long-suffering to the wicked. Therein lie His awful powers: for but for the fear of him, how could one (single) nation persist among the (many) nations.' "

"But how could the Rabbis (Jeremiah and Daniel) abolish something established by Moses? Rabbi Eleazer said: 'Since they knew that the Holy One, blessed be He, insists on truth, they would not ascribe false (things) to him.' " (Talmud Yoma 69b)

Jeremiah and Daniel felt that at that particular time G-d desired to hide His mighty and awful deeds.

No wonder the Rabbis comment on Job's outcry against the divine injustice to him that "One is not held responsible for what he says in time of distress." (Talmud Baba Bathra 16a)

This principle, that one is exempted from expressions made under duress, is also applicable in our legal system. The Talmud (Nedarim, p. 27a), rules that vows made under compulsion and force, have no validity. This is based on scripture. If a man forcibly violates a bethrothed girl in a field where she can get no help, then the girl has no sin. "Unto the girl you shall do nothing; there is in the girl no sin worthy of death; for as when a man rises against his neighbor and slays him, even so in this matter. For he found her in the field; the betrothed girl cried out and there were none to save her." (Deuteronomy 22:26-27)

Acts and expressions resulting from physical force or physical and mental anguish can carry no blame.

Chapter 11

TEXT

*Then answered Zophar the Naamathite and said: Should
not the multitude of words be answered? and should a man
of talk be justified? Your boasting put men to silence and
you scoff with no one to make you ashamed. For you have
said my teaching is pure and I am clean in Your eyes. But,
oh, that G-d would speak and open His lips against you. He
will tell you the secrets of wisdom for there are mysteries in
understanding, and know that G-d makes you forget your
sin. Can you find out the deep things of G-d, or can you attain the purpose of the Almighty? It is high as heaven; what
can you do? Deeper than the nether world—what can you
know? Its measure is longer than the earth and wider than
the sea. If He pass by and imprison, or gather in, who can
hinder Him? For he knows worthless men and when He
sees iniquity He will not overlook it. But a senseless man
will learn when an ass's colt is born a man. If you will direct
your heart and stretch out your hands to Him. If iniquity be
in your hand, put it far away and let no wrong dwell in your
tent. Surely then, you will lift up your face without blemish,
you will be steadfast and you shall not fear. For you shall*

forget your misery, remembering it as waters that have passed away. And life would rise up brighter than noonday, though there be darkness it shall be as the morning. You will be secure because there is hope, you will search and rest in safety. You will lie down with none to frighten you and many would seek to win your favor. But the eyes of the wicked shall fail and refuge will be lost to them; and their hope is an expiring breath.

COMMENTARY

Zophar, roused by Job's replies, attacks him and rebukes him. He draws a picture contrasting the prosperity and happiness of the pious with the adversity and failure of the wicked. It is simple theology. It pays to be good. Be good and material success will follow. Conversely, if you suffer, you have sinned.

Eliphaz indicates the cause of Job's suffering "because no man is perfect." Bildad, a little bolder than Eliphaz, bases his argument on the fact, the "experience and wisdom of man proves that G-d destroys the wicked." Zophar begins with a direct accusation of Job's guilt. Zophar flares up at Job, accusing him that he "mocks the truth," which is the established theology of his day. He resents Job's insistence on his innocence and uprightness as being arrogant and false.

Although Zophar repeats the doctrine of absolute retribution, he develops a new basis. He depicts a colossal contrast between G-d and man. He bases his theology upon a very modern aspect of psychology. Man may sin, but then he becomes oblivious to his actions.

Zophar wants to prove that the divine order is incomprehensible to man. "He will tell you the (hidden) secrets of wisdom for there are mysteries in understanding and know that G-d makes you forget your sin."

The general translation of the last statement is "and know that G-d exacts of you less than your iniquity deserves." Our translation follows Ibn Ezra and Ralbag "that G-d makes you forget your sin," since the verb in this sentence means "obliterates from your memory."

70

Here the author of Job ascribes to G-d not only the act of restricting man's capacity of comprehension, but also man's capacity for forgetfulness. Man's acts are cast into oblivion and thereby he obliterates from memory all his sins.

This thought is repeated in Zophar's appeal to Job that he repent. "Surely then, you will lift up your face without blemish; you will be steadfast and you shall not fear; for you shall forget your misery, remembering it as waters that have passed away." (15,16)

"G-d makes you forget your sin," is Zophar's suggestion to Job. He implies that Job may be suffering for sins he had committed in the past, but by now has forgotten.

The famous Rabbi of Kotsk chose a similar interpretation on the last speech by Moses in Deuteronomy (32:18). "The Rock that begot you, you are unmindful and you have forgotten G-d that gave you birth." The Rabbi continued: "G-d implanted within you the capacity of forgetfulness in order to forget the shallowness and follies of life. In the end, you use the instinct of forgetfulness to forget the very G-d who created you."

Chapters 12, 13 and 14

TEXT: CHAPTER 12

Then Job answered and said: Truly you are the people, and with you wisdom will die. But I also have sense like you, I am not inferior to you, and who does not know all this? I am as one laughed at by his friends who called upon G-d and He answered him; a laughing-stock though righteous and innocent. In the thought of one who is at ease there is contempt for misfortune, ready for those whose foot slips. The tents of robbers prosper, and they who provoke G-d are secure, they who bring their god in their hand. But ask now the beasts and they will teach you; and the birds of the heavens and they will tell you. Or speak to the earth and let it teach you; and the fishes of the sea shall declare to you. Which among all these does not know that the hand of the Lord has done this? In whose hand is the soul of every living thing and the breath of all human beings. Does not the ear try words as the palate tastes its food? Is wisdom with aged men and understanding in length of days? With Him are wisdom and power; He has counsel and understanding. Behold, He destroys and it cannot be rebuilt; He imprisons a man and there can be no opening. Behold, He restrains the waters, they dry up: He sends them out, they overturn the earth. With Him are strength and sound wisdom; His are the deceived and the deceiver. He leads counselors away bereft of sense and judges, He turns into fools. He looses the bonds of kings and binds a girdle on their loins. He leads priests away bereft of sense and overthrows the mighty. He deprives the self-confident of speech and takes away discretion from the elders. He pours contempt upon nobles and the belt of the mighty he looses. He uncovers the depths of darkness and brings to light the shadow of death. He makes nations great and destroys them. He expands the nations and leads them away. He takes away the intelligence of the chiefs of the people of the land and makes them wander in a pathless waste. They grope in the dark with no light, and He makes them wander astray like a drunken man.

TEXT: CHAPTER 13

Behold, all this my eye has seen, my ear has heard and understood it. What you know I know also, I am not inferior to you. However, I would speak to the Almighty and I desire to reason with G-d. But you are inventors of lies, worthless physicians are you all. Oh, that you would indeed be silent that would be wisdom on your part. Hear now my argument and listen to the pleadings of my lips. Is it for G-d that you speak falsely and for His sake will you talk deceitfully? Will you show Him partiality? Will you contend for G-d? Will it be well if He investigates you? Or will you deceive Him as one deceives a man? He will surely rebuke you if you secretly show partiality. Should not His majesty terrify you and His dread fall upon you? Your maxims are proverbs of ashes, your defenses of clay. Keep silent before me that I may speak; let come to me what may. Whatever be, I will take my flesh in my teeth and my life will I take in my hand. Though he slay me yet will I trust in Him; only I will argue my own way before Him. This also shall be my salvation, for a hypocrite cannot come before Him. Listen well to my words and let my declaration be in your ears. Behold now, I drew up my case. I know that

I shall be justified. Who is there to contend with me? Then I would be silent and die. Only two things do not to me, then I will not hide myself from you. Remove Your Hand far from me and let not Your dread terrify me. Then call and I will answer, or I will speak and You answer me. How many are my iniquities and sins? Let me know my transgressions and my sin. Why do you hide Your face and regard me as Your enemy? Will You harass a driven leaf? and will You pursue dry stubble? That You write bitter decrees against me and make me inherit the sins of my youth. You put my feet in the stocks and watch all my parts; You draw a line about the soles of my feet. And he (the person in misfortune) is like rottenness that decays, like a moth eaten garment.

TEXT: CHAPTER 14

Man that is born of woman, is of few days and full of trouble. Like a blossom he comes forth and withers; he flees like a shadow and does not endure. Yet, on such a one, You open Your eyes and bring me to judgment with You. Oh, that a clean thing could come out of an unclean, not one. Since his days are determined, the number of his months is with You, and You have set bounds that he cannot pass. Look away from him that he may rest and be able like a hired laborer, to enjoy his day. For there is hope for a tree if it be cut down, then it will sprout again and its shoots will not cease. If its root becomes old in the ground and its trunk dies in the soil. At the scent of water it will bud and produce boughs like a plant. But man dies and is powerless and man expires and where is he? Like waters gone from the sea, like a river drained dry. So man lies down and does not rise till the heavens be no more. They will not awake and will not be roused out of their sleep. Oh, that You would hide me in the nether world, conceal me till Your wrath be appeased, that You would appoint me a set time and remember me! If a man dies, does he live? All the days of my service I would wait until my turn should come. You would call and I would answer You; You would yearn for the work of Your hands. But now You count my steps.

My transgression is sealed up in a bag and You add to my iniquity. Truly a falling mountain crumbles and a rock moves out of its place. Water wears away stones; its torrents wash away the soil of the earth; so You destroy the hope of man. You prevail forever against him and he passes; You change his appearance and send him away. His children attain honor, but he does not know it and they are brought low, but he does not perceive them. But his flesh upon him has pain and his soul will mourn for him.

COMMENTARY: CHAPTERS 12, 13 and 14

To the student of the Bible, Jonah represents the opposite view of Job in his acceptance of divine justice in the world. Job's protestation against divine injustice reaches a climax in the closing of the first cycle of speeches in this Book. Jonah like Job, prefers death to living, but for the opposite reason. Job pleads for death, "now therefore, take my life," because of divine justice.

Jonah is asked to go to Nineveh and proclaim against its wickedness. Jonah instead flees to Tarshish to avoid this mission. A second call comes from G-d to Jonah. This time he obeys the command. The wicked people accept the warning. They repent and are forgiven. Jonah is reluctant to accept the excessive mercy in the divine order that forgave the extreme wickedness of these people. But Jonah was greatly displeased and angry. So he prayed to the Lord saying: "O Lord, is not this what I said while I was still on my own soil? Therefore I hastened to flee to Tarshish. For I knew you are a gracious G-d, compassionate, long-suffering and abundant in mercy, and relenting of evil. Now therefore, O Lord, take my life from me. For I am better off dead than alive." (Jonah 4:1-4)

Jonah lived during the first half of the eighth century B.C.E. This was a very sinful and calamitous period in Jewish history. Jonah was therefore resentful of the overabundance of G-d's mercy to the sinful people of Nineveh. They were spared the punishment due them for their iniquities. The Bible relates: "In the fifteenth year of Amazioh, the son of Joash King of Judah, Jereboam King of Israel

75

began to rule in Samaria and he reigned forty and one years. And he did that which was evil in the sight of the Lord; he did not depart from all the sins of Jereboam the son of Nvot in that he made Israel to sin. He restored the border of Israel from the entrance of Chamath to the sea of Arabia according to the word of the Lord, the G-d of Israel which He spoke by His servant Jonah the son of Amittai the prophet. For the Lord saw the affliction of Israel that it was very bitter; for there was none shut up nor left at large; neither was there any helper in Israel." (II Kings 14:23-26) Since Jonah witnessed the tragic conditions of his own people, he was outraged that the G-d of justice would condone and forgive the oppressive sins of the people of Nineveh.

The story of a conversation between Moses and G-d further illustrates a reason for the contrasting views of Job and Jonah. This occurred on Moses' first mission to redeem his people from Egypt.

"And Moses said unto G-d: 'When I come unto the children of Israel and say unto them: The G-d of your fathers has sent me to you. And they will say to me, What is His name? What shall I say to them?' " (Exodus 3:13) The Midrash offers G-d's reply which provides us with a greater understanding of Providence and justice.

G-d said to Moses: You want to know My name? *I am called in accordance with My acts in the world.* At times I am called by the name of 'Infinite Might,' 'Lord of Hosts,' 'Lord,' (Elokin) 'G-d' (Hashem). When I deal out strict justice I am called (Elokim) 'Lord.' When I make war with the wicked I am called 'Lord of Hosts.' When I suspend the sins of man I am called 'Infinite-Mighty' and when I exercise mercy upon the world I am called (Hashem) 'G-d.' (Exodus Rabbah 3:6)

Job is puzzled by the mystery of his suffering, and Jonah is stunned by the reprieve of Nineveh.

The daily morning prayer declares G-d as the dispenser of all things. The prayer reads "Who forms light and creates darkness who makes peace and creates all things." This prayer is based on Isaiah (45:6-7). "I am the Lord and there is none else, I form light and create darkness; I make peace and create evil."

"Jewish teaching recognizes that nothing coming from G-d is in itself evil, that even the lower passions may be made agencies for good. Hence the change of 'creates all things.' G-d is the sole source of every thing." (Seder T'Filla Rabbi J. H. Hertz)

Chapter 15

TEXT

Then answered Eliphaz the Temanite and said: Should a wise man utter windy knowledge and fill his belly with the east wind? Should he argue with unprofitable talk and with words of no avail? Indeed you are doing away with fear and diminish devotion before G-d. For your iniquity prompts your speech and you choose the tongue of the crafty. Your own mouth condemns you, not I, and your own lips witness against you. Were you born as the first man? Were you brought forth before the hills? Do you hear the secret council of G-d? And do you restrain wisdom to yourself? What do you know that we do not? What insight have you that we lack? With us are the gray-headed and aged much older than your father. Are the consolations of G-d too trivial for you and the word that was so mild with you? Why does your heart carry you away and why do your eyes flash, that you turn your temper against G-d and utter such words from your mouth? What is man that he should be pure or one born of woman to be righteous? Behold, He puts no trust in His holy ones and the heavens are not pure in His eyes. How much less, one who is abominable and corrupt, man who drinks wrongdoing like water. I will instruct you, listen to me, and that which I have seen I will relate. What the wise declare without concealing from their fathers. To whom alone the land was given and into whose midst no alien passed. All the days of the wicked, he is tormented with pain, and the number of years laid up for the tyrant. Dreadful sounds are in his ears; in the midst of peace the destroyer comes upon him. He does not believe that he will return from the darkness, and he is destined for the sword. He wanders about for bread, where is it? He knows that the day of darkness is ready at hand; distress and anguish terrify him; they overpower him like a king ready for the battle. For his hand he has raised against G-d and is arrogant toward the Almighty. He runs against him with a stubborn stick, with the thick side of his shields. For he has covered his face with his fat and amassed fat upon his loins. And he has dwelt in desolate cities, in houses uninhabited which were destined to be heaps. He shall not be rich nor will his wealth endure, nor will his harvest bend to the ground. He will never depart out of darkness; the flame shall dry up his branches and by the breath of His mouth shall he go away. Let him not trust in falsehood deceiving himself, for falsehood shall be his recompense. Before his time, it will be fulfilled and his branch shall not be green. He will mar like a vine—his unripe grapes, and he will cast, like the olive tree, his blossom. For the assembly of hypocrites will be desolate, and fire devour the tents of bribery. They conceive mischief, and bring forth iniquity, and their belly prepares deceit.

COMMENTARY

Eliphaz now begins the second cycle of speeches, augmented by the words of Bildad and Zophar, Eliphaz repeats, with greater emphasis, the major premise that a terrible and total destruction will come upon the wicked. G-d is just and a just G-d must punish the sinful. This is how they interpret the strict doctrine of reward and punishment.

Eliphaz presents this principle, ignoring the concept of

divine mercy. Instead of depicting man in the image of G-d, they depict G-d in the image of man. The Rabbis present a different view. "The Holy One, Blessed be He, said: 'If I create the world with the quality of mercy there will be many sinners. If I create the world with the quality of strict justice, how will the world be able to exist? I will therefore combine both, justice with mercy.' " "This may be compared to a king who had empty goblets. Said the king, 'If I fill them with hot water they will burst. If I fill them with cold water they will crack. What did he do? He mixed hot and cold water and poured it into these goblets and they remained unimpaired. So, also, G-d created the world by combining the quality of justice with the quality of mercy.' " (Midrash Rabbah Genesis 12:15)

Combining mercy with justice results in delaying punishment of the wicked. The Midrash depicts historical personalities to whom this was applied.

"For three reasons G-d shows forbearance with the wicked in this world. One, perhaps they will repent. Two, perhaps they will do mitzvohs (good deeds) for which G-d can reward them in this world. Three, perhaps upright children will descend from them."

History has proven this. G-d was long-suffering with Ahaz (King of Judah 577-561 B.C.E.), who ruled for sixteen years. He offered his own son to pass through fire worship and introduced idol worship (II Kings 12:3), from whom Hezekiah (King of Judah 561-532 B.C.E.) was a descendent. He ruled for 29 years, destroyed all idol worship and renewed the Temple service and the laws of Moses. (Kings 18:3)

G-d was long-suffering with Shimei (member of King Saul's family who cursed and conspired against King David —II Samuel 16:5) from whom Mordecai was descended. (Mordecai was a hero of the Book of Esther, a steadfast Jew through whom Persian Jewry was saved.) (Midrash Rabbah Ecclesiastes 7:15)

Mordecai's efforts form the central theme of the story of Purim. Long-suffering to Shimei resulted in the birth of Mordecai and his heroic life to save his people.

80

Chapters 16 and 17

TEXT: CHAPTER 16

Then Job replied and said: I have heard many things like these, troublesome comforters are you all. Is there any end to words of wind? or what compels you that you should answer? I too could speak like you, if you were in my place, I could join words together against you and I could shake my head at you. I could strengthen you with my mouth and the moving of my lips would restrain your grief. Though I speak my pain is not restrained, and if I cease, what (burden) departs from me? But now He has made me weary; you have made me desolate, all my company. And you have shriveled me up, it has become a witness, my leanness has risen against me, it testifies to my face. His wrath has torn me and hates me; He has gnashed on me with His teeth; my adversary flashes his eyes upon me. They open wide their mouth against me in scorn, they smite my cheek, they mass themselves against me. G-d delivers me to the unjust and into the hands of the wicked. He surrenders me. I was at ease and he crushed me. He seized me by the neck and smashed me. He set me up as his target. His archers encircle about me; He splits my kidneys without

*mercy. He pours out my gall on the ground. He breaks me
with breath after breath; He runs upon me like a warrior. I
sewed sackcloth upon my skin and I have laid my horn in
the dust. My face is flushed from weeping and on my eyelids
rest the shadow of death. Although there is no violence on
my hands and my prayer is pure, O earth, cover not my
blood. Let my cry find no place to rest. Even now, my
witness is in heaven and He who testifies for me is on high.
Are my friends my defenders? But my eye pours out tears
unto G-d. And oh, that a man might plead with G-d even
as a man with his friend. For when numbered years are
passed then must I travel a path that I shall not return.*

TEXT: CHAPTER 17

*My spirit is broken, my days are cut short, the grave
is ready for me. Surely mockery surrounds me and my eye
dwells on their defiance. Give, now a surety for me with
Yourself, who else is there that will strike hands with me?
For You have closed their minds against reason, therefore
You will not exalt them. He who speaks deceptively to his
friends, the eyes of his children will fail. He has made me a
byword unto nations and I am become one before whom
men spit. My eye is dim because of grief and my limbs are
all like a shadow. The upright are amazed at this and the
innocent must arouse himself against the hypocrite. But the
righteous will hold to his way, and he who has clean hands
will grow stronger and stronger. But all of you, return and
come now; I shall not find a wise man among you. My
days have passed on; my reserves are broken, even the
thoughts of my heart. They turn night into day, the light as
near in the presence of darkness. When I hope for the nether
world as my home, I spread out my couch in the darkness.
I have called the pit: "you are my father" and to the worm
"you are my mother and sister." Where then is my hope
and as for my hope who will see it? They shall go down to
the gates of the nether world, verily in the dust there is
rest for all.*

COMMENTARY: CHAPTERS 16 and 17

Jeremiah, like Job, cried out in bitterness "Woe is me, my mother that you have borne me, a man of strife and a man of contention to the whole earth. I have not lent, neither have men lent to me, yet every one of them curses me. (Jeremiah 15:10) For as often as I speak, I cry out, I cry: violence and spoil; because the word of the Lord is made a reproach unto me, and a derision all the day. Cursed be the day wherein I was born; the day whereon my mother bore me, let it not be blessed. Wherefore came I forth out of the womb to see labor and sorrow that my days would be consumed in shame." (Jeremiah 20:8, 14, 18)

Jeremiah was predestined to prophesy during 40 years which were a period of black disaster. Like Job, he was the unwilling tool in the hands of Providence. "And I knew you and before you came forth out of the womb I sanctified you; I have appointed you a prophet unto the nations.' Then I said, 'Oh Lord G-d, behold I cannot speak for I am a child.' " But the Lord said unto me: 'Say not "I am a child.' For to whomsoever I shall send you, you should go; and whatsoever I shall command you, you shall speak.' " (Jeremiah 1:4-7)

At the risk of his life, Jeremiah proclaimed that "Unless the people repent, the nation and even the Temple will be destroyed." For this prophecy, he was arraigned on the capital charge of treason. If not for the intervention of the princes, he would have been executed.

Jeremiah, like Job, suffered physically and mentally. Like Job he became the target of his friends and even his family. Like Job he dares to ask questions of theodicy reconciling existence of evil with divine justice. "You are righteous, O Lord, were I to contend with You. Yet will I reason with you. Why does the way of the wicked prosper? Why do all the faithless live in comfort? You plant them and they take root. They grow and they bring forth fruit near are you in their mouths, but far from their thoughts." (Jeremiah 12:1-3)

Like Job, Jeremiah may be puzzled by the events of his day, but he never lost faith. "O Lord, my strength and my stronghold, my refuge in the day of affliction." (Jeremiah 17:7)

In the midst of his misery and the derision of his friends, Job also says "Even now, my witness is in heaven and He who testifies for me is on high. My friends scorn me but my eye pours out tears to G-d." (Job 16:19-20) The Baal Shem Tov in his book *Tifereth Yehudah* speaks of faith as surpassing reason. Here follows the excerpt from his book.

"We learn in the Talmud (Rosh Hashona p. 21) that forty-nine out of fifty levels of reason were given to Moses. But since man yearns to know more, how did Moses continue to study? The answer is that when he found the fiftieth level too complex and unapproachable by the human mind he substituted faith and meditated further upon those aspects of knowledge open to him. In this way, everybody ought to discipline his mind. He should study and reflect to the utmost of his ability. When he reaches a point where he is unable to comprehend further, he may substitute faith, then return to the learning that is within his grasp."

Dr. Aron Barth, in his book *The Modern Jew Faces Eternal Problems* asks "Can science explain the very beginning of creation?" The answer is "no." Scientific research into the manner in which the universe came into existence has been renewed in recent years. In every serious book on such research it is said explicit or implicity "We can bring you up to a certain point, with a greater or smaller measure of certainty, but beyond that point we cannot go." Further, he says, "If, therefore, we want an answer to the question, 'What is the origin of matter and energy we must transcend the world of nature and consider the time when nature and its laws were not in existence.' We learn, therefore, that science cannot answer our question."

Prof. M. Smart, astronomer Royal in Glasgow warns his readers not to fall into the erroneous belief that science can answer these ultimate questions. In his book *The Origin of the Earth* he writes: "There may be, and I think there is, a point in the remote past where an 'iron wall' of cosmic fabrication shuts us out from scientific contemplation of the antecedent state and primeval evolutionary history of the universe.

"We are concerned, then, in this book, with the study of the past, pressing as far back as our means permit, and perhaps coming in sight of a barrier, as already suggested, beyond which it would seem we cannot pass." "Perhaps, here, we may ask, legitimately, if in probing in the deepest sense of the mystery of creation, science has really been more successful than the poetic expounder of Hebrew cosmogony. The answer seems to be emphatically, 'No'."

Chapter 18

TEXT

Then Bildad the Shuhite replied and said: When will you at length put an end to words? Understand and afterward we will speak. Why are we accounted as beasts? reputed stupid in your eyes? You, who tear yourself in your anger, shall the earth be forsaken for you, or the rock be moved from its place? Verily, the light of the wicked goes out and the flame of his fire shall not give light. The light grows dark in his tent and the lamp above him goes out. His strong steps are shortened and his own counsel will cast him down. For he is driven to his net by his own feet and he walks upon a pitfall. A trap seizes him by the heel; a snare lays hold upon him. A noose is concealed for him in the ground and a trap is set for him in the pathway. All around terrors scare him and shall entrap him at his feet. His strength (first born) will suffer hunger and calamity will be ready for his side (his wife). It will devour the limbs of his body, the first born of death will devour his limbs. He is snatched away from his tent, in which he trusted, and he will be brought to the king of terrors. There will dwell in his tent nothing of his; brimstone will be scattered upon his habitation. Beneath his roots will be dried up and above his branch will be cut off. His remembrance will vanish from the earth and no name remains for him abroad. They shall drive him from light into darkness; they shall chase him from the world. He shall have neither son nor grandson among his people, nor any remaining in his dwellings. Coming generations will be astonished over his day and those that were before him, were frightened. Such is the fate that befalls the homes of the wicked and such is the place of him who knows not G-d.

COMMENTARY

Bildad begins by disputing Job's contention that the wicked prosper. To the contrary, he depicts the multiple evils that befall the wicked. If you read this chapter carefully you will find ten expressions for snares and traps by which the wicked are brought to disaster and destruction.

Bildad's concept of divine justice includes "His (wicked) roots shall dry up beneath and above shall his branch wither" (16). This is a metaphoric expression that his entire family will perish with him. And "He shall have neither son nor grandson among his people, nor any remaining in his dwellings." (19)

The punishment, suffering and extinction of the children of the wicked are part of Bildad's world order. This is contrary to the prophetic declarations of Jeremiah and Ezekiel.

"In those days shall they say no more the fathers have eaten sour grapes and the children's teeth are set on edge; but everyone shall die for his own guilt, everyone who eats the sour grapes shall have his own teeth set on edge." (Jeremiah 31:28-30)

"His father died for his iniquity because he practiced oppression, robbed his fellow man, and did what was evil among his people; and you ask, 'Why should not the son bear the consequences of his father's iniquity?' If the son do what is lawful and right, by being careful to observe all My statutes, he shall surely live. He who sins shall die; the son shall not bear the consequences of the father's iniquity, nor the father bear the consequences of the son's iniquity; the righteousness of the righteous shall be put to his own account and the wickedness of the wicked shall be put to his." (Ezekiel 18:18-21)

The prophetic expressions are based on Biblical law. "The fathers shall not be put to death for the children, neither shall the children be put to death for the fathers; every man shall be put to death for his own sin." Deut. 24:16

In contrast to this concept of personal responsibility, we find collective responsibility in ancient legal codes. We find cases where entire tribes or an entire family was held responsible for an act of murder by a member of that tribe or family.

In the Code of Hammurabi, who lived about the time of Abraham, about 2000 B.C.E., we find a law, "Son for a son, daughter for a daughter." This retaliation principle is carried to grotesque extremes. For example, if the jerry-builder, by his faulty construction of a house, causes the death of the son or daughter of the owner, then not the jerry-builder, but his son or daughter is killed . . . The Torah sweeps away an infamous caricature of human justice. (Hertz: Exodus p. 289)

Chapter 19

TEXT

Then Job answered and said: How long will you grieve my soul and crush me with words. These ten times have you reproached me; you are not ashamed to act as strangers to me. And if it be indeed that I erred let my error remain with myself. But if indeed you wish to magnify yourselves above me and, to prove against me, my disgrace, then know that G-d has bent me down and has enclosed me in his net. Behold, I cry out violence, but I am not heard, I cry aloud, but there is no justice. My way has He fenced up that I cannot pass and upon my paths he set darkness. He has stripped me of my glory and removed the crown of my head. He has broken me down on every side and I am gone; and my hope he has uprooted like a tree. He has kindled his wrath against me and regards me as one of the adversaries to Him. His troops come on together and make their level way against me and encamp round about my tent. He has put my brothers far from me and my friends are entirely estranged from me. My relatives have withdrawn and my intimates have forgotten me. The guests of my house and my maids regard me as a stranger, an alien I became in their eyes. I call my servant, but he will not answer, though I implore him with my mouth. My breath is offensive to my wife, and I am loathsome to the children of my tribe. Even young children despise me; I rise up, they speak against me. All that had my confidence abhor me, and those whom I loved have turned against me. My bones cling to my skin and to my flesh, and I am escaped with the gums of my teeth. Have pity on me, have pity on me, O you, my friends, for the hand of G-d has touched me. Why do you persecute me like G-d, and are not satisfied with my flesh? Oh, that my words were now written! Oh, that they were inscribed in a book! That with an iron pen and lead they were graven in the rock forever! But as for me I know that my Redeemer lives and that at last He will remain as a witness upon the dust. Even after my skin has been torn from my flesh, freed from my flesh, shall I see G-d. Whom I, even I, shall see for myself and whom my eyes will see to be no stranger, my reins yearn within me. But if you should say 'how will we pursue him, seeing that the root of the matter is found in me." (The answer) Be afraid of the sword for the (divine) wrath brings the sword and you will know that there is judgment.

COMMENTARY

Habakuk, the prophet (about 600 B.C.E.) asks the same questions as Job in this chapter, about the apparent injustice in the world. He uses the identical language, and he similarly awaits an answer from on High.

Job says: "Behold, I cry out 'Violence,' but I am not heard, I cry out loud, but there is no justice." (7)

Habakuk says: "How long, O Lord, shall I cry and you will not hear? I cry out unto you 'violence' and you will not save. Why do You show me iniquity and make me see mischief? Destruction and violence are before me, and there is strife; and contention arises. Therefore the law is paralyzed and judgment never goes forth. But the wicked circumvent the righteous, therefore judgment goes forth perverted." (1:2-5)

"Too pure of eye are You to behold evil. And You cannot look on mischief. Why then do You gaze upon faithless men and keep silent when the wicked swallows up the man that is more righteous than he. For you make men like fish of the sea, like reptiles with no ruler." (Habakuk 1:13-15)

Also like Job, Habakuk awaits an answer from G-d.

"I will stand upon my watch, and station myself upon the tower, and watch to see what He will say to me and what reply I shall bring back about my complaint." (Habakuk 2:1)

In this chapter Job expresses his lofty trust in G-d. In spite of the condemnation of his friends and the torment of his physical afflictions, Job remains steadfast in his faith in G-d.

Job begins to see significance in his suffering. He says: "Oh, that my words were now written! Oh, that they were inscribed in a book! That with an iron pen and lead they were graven in the rock forever! But as for me, I know that my Redeemer lives." (23-25)

This last phrase demonstrates Job's victory of faith. Job wishes to record his experience. Habakuk is told to inscribe his vision.

"And the Lord answered me and said: 'Write the vision clearly upon the tablets that one may read on the run. For the vision is still for the appointed time and declares for the end and does not lie; though it tarry, wait for it; for it will surely come, it will not delay. Verily his soul is puffed up, it is not upright in him; *but the righteous lives by his faith.*" (Habakuk 2:2-5)

Habakuk proclaims the conclusion that you have to believe even if you don't understand the divine order of the world.

There is a deep similarity between the Books of Job and Habakuk. Both begin by protesting, challenging and questioning G-d's justice. Both end in a crescendo of deathless faith. Habakuk concludes that the "righteous lives by his faith" and Job says, "I know my Redeemer lives."

Rabbi Akiva demonstrated a very deep faith in G-d's

justice. Whatever happened to him, even if it appeared evil or as a misfortune, he still said: "What G-d does is for good."

Once he was traveling and he came to a certain town. He looked for lodging but was refused it everywhere. He said, "Whatever G-d does is for good." He had to spend that night in an open field. He had with him a hen, a donkey and a lamp. A strong wind came and blew out the lamp; a weasel came and ate the hen; a lion came and devoured the donkey. Even then he said: "Whatever G-d does is for the good." The same night robbers came and captured the inhabitants of the town. He then remarked, "Did I not say whatever G-d does is for the good." The light of the lamp and the sounds of the hen and donkey would have betrayed his presence to the robbers. (Talmud Brochot 60b)

Chapter   20

TEXT

*Then Zophar the Naamathite replied, saying: There-
fore my thoughts answer me; and because of the agitation
within me. I hear the rebuke that would put me to shame,
yet out of my understanding, my spirit will answer me. Do
you know this as from old times, since man was placed on
earth, that the triumph of the wicked is but short and the
joy of the hypocrite but for a moment. Though his exal-
tation mount up to the heavens and his head reach the
clouds, he will perish forever like his own dung; those
who saw him will say 'where is he?' Like a dream he will
fly away as a vision of the night. The eye that saw him
will see him no more, nor will he be seen in his place. His
children will seek favor from the poor and his own hands
will give back his wealth. His bones are full of youth, but
will lie down with him in the dust. If evil be sweet in his
mouth as he keeps it and withhold it in his palate. His food
in his bowels is turned into poison of asps within him. The
wealth which he swallowed he will have to vomit up, G-d
will drive it out of his belly. He sucks the poison of asps,
the tongue of the adder will slay him. He shall not look*

upon the streams on flowing brooks of honey and curds.
He gives back that which he labored for, and will not
swallow it. He does not rejoice in proportion of his gain.
For he has oppressed and forsaken the poor, and robbed a
house he shall not rebuild. Because he knew not quietness
within him he shall save nothing of that which he de-
lights. Nothing was left from his craving to devour, there-
fore his prosperity will not endure. In the fullness of his
abundance distress will be upon him; every hand he troubled
will come against him. Let it be for the filling of his belly
that He cast the fury of his wrath upon him and rain down
his anger upon him. He will flee from the weapon of iron,
and the bow of bronze will pierce him. He draws it and it
comes out of his back, and the glittering sword out of his
gall, terror comes upon him. All darkness is stored up for
his treasure; a fire that is not blown will devour him; it will
destroy anyone that is left in his tent. The heavens will
disclose his iniquity and the earth will rise up against him.
The products of his house shall depart flowing away on
the day of His wrath. This is the lot of a wicked man from
G-d, and his decreed heritage from G-d.

COMMENTARY

Zophar depicts the downfall and punishment of the
wicked. He emphasizes the horror and terror that is the lot
of the wicked. But the concept of immediate and total
reward and punishment in this world is not correct Jewish
doctrine. It is true that reward and punishment is a cardinal
principle of religion. The belief in retribution forms the
eleventh of the thirteen articles of faith by Maimonides. "I
firmly believe that the Creator, blessed be His name, rewards those who keep his commands, and punishes those
who transgress His commands."

In the Bible the promises, both of reward and punishment, that are of a material and worldly nature, are intended primarily for the nation as a whole, and only
occasionally are addressed to the individual.

Zophar and his friends fail to convince Job because
their dogmatic doctrine of immediate retribution is neither

true to life nor sound religious training. Judaism teaches that neither reward nor punishment is always carried out in this world. The Mishna states "If you have studied much Torah much reward will be given to you. The master of your task is faithful to pay you the reward for your work; but know that the reward of the righteous will be in the world to come." (Avoth 2:21)

"These are the things which man must perform and he enjoys their fruit in this world while the principal remains for him in the world to come: They are: honoring father and mother; the practice of kind deeds and making peace between man and his fellow man: but the study of Torah surpasses them all." (Talmud: Sabbath 27a)

"Every day, a heavenly voice is heard declaring: 'The whole world draws its sustenance because (of the merit) of Hanina my son and Hanina my son suffices himself with a "kab" (2.2 litres) of carobs from one Sabbath to another.' Every Friday his wife would light the oven and throw twigs into it, (to produce smoke) so as not to be put to shame by others knowing of their hunger.

"Once his wife said to him, 'How long shall we go on suffering so much?' He replied; 'what shall we do?' 'Pray that something be given to you.' He prayed and there emerged the figure of a hand holding out to him the leg of a golden table. But he saw in a dream that the pious would one day eat at a three-legged table and he at a two legged table. He said to his wife 'Are you satisfied that everybody shall eat at a perfect table and we eat at an imperfect table?' She replied 'What then shall we do!' 'Pray that the leg shall be taken away from you.' He prayed and it was taken away." (Talmud Taanith 24b)

Since no human being is ever perfectly pious nor totally wicked, it may be that the pious suffer in this world and they receive their full reward in the world to come.

Maimonides cites many views of punishment in the hereafter, but his own view he expresses as follows: "Know that just as a blind man can form no idea of colors, nor a deaf man comprehend sound, so the body cannot comprehend the delights of the soul. Even as fish do not know the element of fire, because they exist ever in the opposite, so are the delights of the world of the spirit unknown in the world of flesh. Indeed, we have no pleasure in any way except what is bodily and what the senses can comprehend, of eating and drinking or the reproductive functions. Whatever is outside these, is nonexistent to us. We do not discern, neither do we grasp it at first thought, but only after deep concentration. And truly this must necessarily be the case. For we live in a material world and the only pleasures we can comprehend must be material. But the delights of the spirit are everlasting and uninterrupted. and there is no resemblance in any possible way between spiritual and bodily enjoyment."—Maimonides' commentary on Mishna. Introduction to Sanhedrin Chapter 10

Chapter 21

TEXT

Then Job replied, saying: Listen attentively to my speech and let this be your consolation. Bear with me while I speak and after I have spoken, mock on. As for me, is my complaint to man? If so, why should I not be impatient. Turn to me and be astonished and lay your hand upon your mouth. Even when I think of it I am terrified and trembling seizes my flesh. Why do the wicked live, grow old and attain great power? Their descendants are established in their presence with them and their offspring before their eyes. Their houses are at peace without fear and the rod of G-d is not upon them. His bull breeds without fail; his cow calves without miscarriage. They send forth their little ones like a flock and their children dance. They sing to the timbrel and harp and rejoice at the sound of the pipe. They spend their days in prosperity and in a moment they go down to the grave.' Yet they say to G-d, "depart from us, we do not want to know your ways. What is the Almighty that we should serve him? and what does it profit us that we pray to Him? Behold, their prosperity is not in their power; the counsel of the wicked is far from me. How often is it that the lamp of the wicked goes out and that their calamity comes upon them; that He distributes their lot in His anger? That they are like straw before the wind, and as chaff that the storm carries away? G-d stores up his wrongdoings for his sons." Let Him punish the man himself that he may know it. Let his own see his destruction and let him drink of the wrath of the Almighty. For what does he care about his house after him when the number of his months is determined. 'Can anyone teach G-d knowledge; it is He who judges the highest. This one dies in his full strength being wholly at ease and satisfied. His vessels are full of milk, and the marrow of his bones is moistened. And another dies in bitterness of soul, and never having enjoyed happiness. In the dust they lie down together and the worm will cover them. Behold, I know your thoughts and the opinions which you wrongfully imagine against me. For you say, "where is the house of the noble and where is the tent in which the wicked dwell? Have you not asked those who travel? You cannot disregard their evidence. That the evil man is spared to the day of calamity, that they are led away on the day of wrath. Who declares his way to his face? or repays him for what he has done? For he will be carried to the grave and watch is kept over his tomb. Sweet to him are the clods of the valley and all men follow after him, even as they were innumerable before him. How then do you comfort me in vain? As for your answers, there remains only deception.

COMMENTARY

Job concludes the second cycle of speeches emphasizing the idea that the wicked live in prosperity. He contradicts their contention that material retributive justice prevails. He insists that the grim facts of life belie his friends' explanation of suffering. Job admits he is puzzled and mystified by G-d's providence.

There is a striking similarity between Job's questions on theodicy and the Psalmist's. Frequently both use the same expressions, except the Psalms provide an answer.

"G-d of retribution, Lord G-d of retribution appear,

rise up, O judge of the earth, render to the arrogant what they deserve. How long shall the wicked, O Lord, how long shall the wicked exult? They gush out, they speak arrogantly; all the workers of iniquity act boastfully. They crush your people, O Lord, and afflict your heritage. They slay the widow and the stranger and murder the orphan. And they say 'The Lord does not see; the G-d of Jacob does not observe.' " (Psalm 94:1-8)

"For I was envious of the arrogant, when I saw the prosperity of the wicked. For they have no pangs at their death and their body is sound. They are not in trouble like other men. Hence pride is as a chain around their neck; a robe of violence covers them. Their eyes stand forth from fatness; they transcend the imagination of the heart. They scoff and speak evil in oppression; they talk as if there were none on high. They have set their mouth against heaven and their tongue wanders over the earth. Therefore His people return here, and waters of fullness are drained out by them. And they say: 'How does G-d know? And is there knowledge in the most High? Behold, such are the wicked and in perpetual ease they amass wealth. Surely in vain have I kept my heart pure, and washed my hands in innocence. For I have been plagued all day long and chastened every morning. If I had said: I will speak this: I should have betrayed the generation of your children. And when I pondered how to understand this, it was a troublesome task in my eyes.' " (Psalms 73:3-16)

The answer to the problem dawned upon the Psalmist as the Psalm continues; "Until I entered into the sanctuary of G-d, then I perceived their end." (17) In the serenity of the sanctuary the solution dawned upon him that he must look beyond their present happy time to the time when the wicked meet their destruction. The Psalmist then can express his deep faith "Whom have I in heaven but You? And having You, I desire none on earth." (25)

To the second question, that the wicked act and say "G-d does not see" the Psalmist offers "Does He who planted the ear not hear? Or He who formed the eye not see?"

(Psalms 94:9) Surely He who gave others the power to hear and see, hears and sees Himself.

The Psalmist realized that human perception is restricted in time; that an occurrence in a man's lifetime might not be an action but a reaction to some occurrence that happened long ago. The Psalmist then says: "The judgments of the Lord are true, they are righteous altogether." Could we but live to see the evolvement from beginning to end we might then comprehend the judgments of G-d.

In this closing speech of the second part of the debate, Job still clings to his view of the apparent success of evil. Later when G-d answers from the whirlwind, Job would join the Psalmist in teaching man not to despair as he sees or experiences suffering.

"Happy is the man whom you train by discipline and whom you teach out of your law" (Psalms 94:14). "Before I was afflicted I did err, but now I observe your word" (Psalms 119:67). "It is good for me that I have been afflicted, in order that I might learn your statutes" (Psalms 119:71)

Chapter 22

TEXT

Then Eliphaz the Temanite answered and said: Can man be profitable to G-d? Surely he who is wise is profitable to himself. Is it any advantage to the Almighty that you are righteous? Or is it of any gain to Him that you should make your ways perfect? Is it because of your piety that He reproves you and enters into judgment with you? Is not your wickedness great? There is no end to your guilt. For you have taken pledges of your brothers for nothing and stripped the naked of their clothing. You have not given water to the weary to drink; and you withheld bread from the hungry. As a man of strong arm he obtained the land and the highly honored could dwell in it. Widows you have sent away empty and the arms of the orphans have been crushed. Therefore snares are around about you and sudden dread will terrify you. Or darkness so that you cannot see and a flood of water will cover you. Is not G-d in the height of heaven? And see the topmost stars, how high they are! Yet you say, "What does G-d know? Can He judge through the dark cloud? Thick clouds conceal Him so that He cannot see, and He walks on the circle of heaven. Will you keep to the path of old which wicked men have trodden; who were snatched away before their time whose foundation was poured out like a river." Who said to G-d, "depart from us" and what can the Almighty do to them? Yet he filled their houses with good things. The counsel of the wicked is far from me. The righteous will see it and be glad and the innocent will scoff at them. Is not he destroyed who rose against us and their surplus the fire has devoured. Acquaint yourself now with Him and be at peace, thereby happiness will come to you. Please accept instruction from His mouth and place His words in your heart. If you will return to the Almighty you will be built up; if you put injustice far from your tent. And throw down in the dust precious metals and the gold of Ophir to the stones of the brooks. And the Almighty will be your treasure and your shining silver. For then you will delight yourself in the Almighty and you will lift up your face unto G-d. You will pray to Him and He will hear you, and you will fulfill your vows. You will decide a matter and it will stand for you, and light will shine upon your ways. When they are brought low you will say "pride," and will save him who is lowly of eyes. He will deliver even him that is not innocent; he will be delivered by the purity of your hands.

COMMENTARY

In opening the third cycle of the debate, Eliphaz persists in finding a reason for Job's suffering.

"Can man be profitable to G-d? Is it any advantage to the Almighty that you are righteous. Is it because of your piety that He reproves you and enters into judgment with you." (2-4) As a friend, Eliphaz should not have overlooked the reputation of Job. Nevertheless, Eliphaz invents lies and raises accusations of definite sins. "Is not your wickedness great? There is no end to your guilt. For you have taken pledges of your brothers for nothing and stripped the naked of their clothing. You have not given water to the weary to drink; and you withheld bread from the hungry. . . Widows you have sent away empty and the arms of the orphans have been crushed." (5-9) "Yet you say,

'What does G-d know, can He judge through dark clouds?' "
(13) All this is not true since Job persists in his faith in G-d in spite of his affliction.

Eliphaz must somehow find a reason for Job's suffering. Job is being punished for sins. Should Job suffer without any reason, then the same can happen to him.

By assigning the reason of sin for Job's suffering, Eliphaz gains both security and peace of mind. Being self righteous with no feeling of guilt, he subconsciously clears himself of such possible tragic fate as befell Job.

In this speech Eliphaz loses his temper. The story is told of an oversatisfied wolf roaming through the forest who wants to prove his power. First a rabbit passes by and the wolf demands "who is the strongest animal in the world?" The trembling rabbit replies: "You are." Then the wolf sees a fox and asks the same question; the clever fox answers "Of course you are." With these declarations the wolf has the illusion of being all-powerful. Just then a huge lion rumbles past and the wolf, forgetful of all reality, asks the lion teasingly, "Who is the strongest animal in the world?" The lion, incensed, gives the wolf a dizzying blow and goes his way. When the wolf regained his composure from the fall, he yells back to the lion "Just because you don't know the answer you don't have to lose your temper!"

Chapters 23 and 24

TEXT: CHAPTER 23

Then Job answered and said: Even today is my complaint bitter; my affliction exceeds my groaning. Oh, that I knew where I might find Him, that I might come to His judgment throne. I would prepare my case before Him and I would fill my mouth with arguments. I would know the words He would answer me, and understand what He would say to me. Would He contend with me in His great power? No, but He would pay heed to me. There the upright might reason with Him, so I should be acquitted by my judge forever. Behold, I go forward, but He is not there; and backward but I cannot perceive him. On the left hand, He is concealed and I cannot behold Him; He wraps Himself in the right that I cannot see Him. For He knows my manner of life; when He has tested me I shall come forth like gold. My foot has held fast to His step; I have kept to His way, and not turned aside. I have not gone back from the commandments of His lips; more than what I apportioned for myself have I treasured the words of His mouth. He is unchangeably One and who can turn Him? What His will desires He does. He will bring to completion that which has been destined for me; and many such things are with Him. Therefore I am terrified at His presence; when I reflect, I am afraid of Him. But G-d has weakened my heart; and the Almighty has overwhelmed me. Because I was not cut off before the darkness, nor did He cover the thick darkness from my face.

TEXT: CHAPTER 24

Why are not sessions (of judgment) set up by the Almighty? And why have not those who know Him seen His days (of retribution)? They remove landmarks, they steal flocks and pasture them. They drive away the donkey of the orphan, they take the widow's ox for a pledge. They crowd the needy off the road, the poor of the land hide themselves together. Indeed, like wild asses in the desert, they go to their task seeking food; the desert yields them bread for the children. They reap the fodder in the field and they glean the vineyard of the wicked. They spend the night naked without clothing and they have no covering in the cold. They are drenched by the rain from the mountains, and cling to the rock for shelter. They snatch the orphan from the breast, and take in pledge that which is on the poor. Naked they go about without clothing, and hungry they carry sheaves. Between the olive rows they press out oil; they tread the wine-presses, but are thirsty. Out of a populous city, groaning is heard, and the soul of the wounded cries out, yet G-d regards it not as an offense. They are those who rebel against the light, they do not know its ways, nor do they dwell in its path. At daylight, the murderer arises that he may kill the poor and the needy; and in the night he is like the thief. The eye of the adulterer watches for the twilight, saying, "No eye shall see me;" and he puts a disguise upon his face. He digs through houses in the darkness; by day they shut themselves up; they do not know light. For the shadow of death (midnight) is to all of them as morning for they are familiar with the terror of the shadow of death. Swiftly he passes on the face of the waters, cursed is their portion in the land; he does not turn toward the way of the vineyard. Drought and heat snatch away snow water; so does the nether world those who have sinned. The womb (his mother) will forget him; the worm will feed sweetly on him; he is no longer remembered and wickedness is broken like a tree. He mistreats the barren, childless woman and shows no kindness to the widow. He draws the mighty by his power, he rises up and no one is sure of life. He grants him security and he is sustained; and His eyes are upon their ways. They are exalted for a little while and they are no more; they are brought low, like all others are they gathered in, and like the top of the ear of corn they are cut off. If it is not so who will prove me a liar and make my speech worthless.

COMMENTARY: CHAPTERS 23 and 24

Job says: "Oh, that I know where I might find Him, that I might come to His judgment throne" (23-1). "Behold, I go forward but He is not there; and backward but I cannot perceive Him. On the left hand He is concealed and I can not behold Him, He wraps Himself in the right that I can not see Him." (23:8-9)

Job's personal search for G-d is so well reflected in this historical episode of Moses' life. Moses was called by G-d to go to Pharaoh, King of Egypt, to release the Israelites from slavery. Unsuccessful in his mission, Moses is blamed by the Hebrew officers that, instead of his promised deliverance, the bondage became more cruel than it was before. This dual disappointment, the failure to bring relief and the blame of his own people, causes Moses to cry out to G-d. Like Job, Moses by reason of his faith, seeks to penetrate the mysteries of the Almighty.

"Then Moses returned again to the Lord and said: O, Lord, why have you brought evil on this people? Why did you send me? Ever since I came to Pharaoh to speak in Your name, he has ill-treated this people and You did not deliver Your people at all."

The Lord said to Moses, "Now you shall see what I will do to Pharaoh, for by a strong hand he shall let them go, and through a strong hand he shall drive them out of his land." (Exodus 5:22 - 6:1) Moses accepts this reassurance of G-d's promise. But Moses seeks a deeper insight into the mysteries of Divine rule. Following the tragic episodes of the wandering in the desert, the golden calf, and the threat of annihilation of the people, Moses presents a request. "If I have found favor in your eyes, pray let me have insight into your ways." (Exodus 33:13)

Then follows G-d's answer. "I will make all my goodness pass before your view, and will proclaim the name of the Lord before you; and I will be gracious to whom I will be gracious and I will show mercy on whom I will show mercy." And He said "You cannot see my face, for man cannot see Me and live." And the Lord said "Here is a place by Me. Station yourself on the rock. When My glory passes by, I will shelter you in a cleft of the rock and will cover you with My hand until I shall have passed by. Then I will take away My hand so that you may see My back, but My face shall not be seen." (Exodus 33:19-23)

The Midrash explains that Moses asked the most perplexing question in the world. Why do the wicked prosper and the righteous suffer? G-d replies that no man can see Him and live. However, the incident of being in the cleft of the rock being covered by the hand of G-d until He has passed, teaches us an obvious lesson. Man cannot see G-d in passing, man can only see where He has passed.

That is the final answer to Moses, and it applies to Job and to all men. We can neither see nor understand G-d's ways as they occur. We can, however, see the footprints of G-d's actions in nature, in man and in history.

The following story of Rabbi Joshua and the prophet Elijah further illustrates this thought. We are unable to perceive the reason or outcome of an event at the time when it happens.

Rabbi Joshua ben Levi and Elijah the prophet were traveling together. They reached the home of a poor man whose entire fortune consisted of one cow. The family was cordial and gave them food and lodging.

In the morning, Elijah prayed that the cow should die. The cow, the only possession of the family, expired.

In the evening they arrived at the home of a very rich

man who refused to receive them. Elijah uttered a blessing and a prayer that a broken wall be miraculously rebuilt in this house.

In the evening they came to a Synagogue where they were received most discourteously. Elijah blessed the congregation and prayed that they all become leaders.

The next day they went to another Synagogue where they were received with honor and respect. The people provided a feast and lodging for them. On leaving, Elijah the prophet blessed them and said: "May the Lord grant you only one leader."

Rabbi Joshua could no longer suffer the unfair and unjust treatment dealt out by Elijah the prophet. Elijah said, "Now I can explain all that seemed so unjust and unreasonable to you. That day the hostess in the poor family was to die, and I prayed the cow die in her place.

"In the house of that rich man there lies buried a great treasure. If the rich man were to rebuild the wall himself he would have discovered that fortune. The congregation that mistreated us, I wished that they all become leaders. For then they will always have strife that will lead to destruction. For the congregation that received us well, I prayed for one leader who would coordinate their activities and unite the people in harmony."

—Sefer Massioth, L'Rabbinu Nissim Gaon

Chapter 25

Then Bildad the Shuhite replied, saying, Dominion and fear are with Him; He makes peace in His high places. Is there any number to His hosts? And on whom does His light not arise? How then can man be justified with G-d or how can he be pure that is born of a woman? Verily, even the moon has no brightness and the stars are not pure in His sight. How much less man that is a worm and the son of man that is a maggot.

COMMENTARY

In his third speech Bildad uses just several sentences contrasting the undisputed supremacy of G-d with the lowest description of man. The sense of this argument can best be summarized in the expression of the Book of Ecclesiastes (7:20): "For no man on earth is righteous who always does good and never sins."

Eliphaz said: "What is man that he should be pure and he that is born of a woman, that he should be righteous. Lo, He puts no trust in His Holy ones, and the heavens are not pure in His eyes; how much less one who is abominable and

109

impure; a man who drinks iniquity like water." (15:14-16)

Bildad briefly depicts the human being with the weakness of his mortal body compelled by motives, passions and physical urges. He can neither be faultless nor is he able to pass judgment on Providence. "How can a man be justified with G-d or how can he be pure that is born of a woman? Behold, even the moon has no brightness and the stars are not pure in His eyes, how much less man, that is a worm, and the son of man, that is a maggot." (25:4-6)

Chapters 26 and 27

TEXT: CHAPTER 26

Then Job answered and said: How you have helped him who is without power and how you saved the arm without strength? How you have counselled him who has no wisdom and abundantly declared sound wisdom. Whom have you told words? And whose spirit came from you. The departed tremble underneath the waters and their inhabitants. The nether world is naked before Him and the lower world has no covering (from His eyes). He stretches out the north over empty space and suspends the earth over nothingness. He binds up the waters in His clouds and the cloud does not burst under their weight. He closed up the surface of His throne spreading over it His cloud. He drew a circle over the face of the waters to the confines of light and darkness. The pillars of heaven tremble and are astonished at His rebuke. By His power, He split the sea and by His understanding, He crushed (its) pride. By His breath, the heavens are serene; His hands pierced the fleeing serpent. Behold, these are but the outer edges of His ways; only a whisper of Him do we catch; who can perceive the thunder of His omnipotence.

111

TEXT: CHAPTER 27

And Job continued to take up his parable and said: As G-d lives who has removed justice from me and the Almighty, who has embittered my soul. As long as my breath is still with me and the spirit of G-d in my nostrils; my lips shall not speak any wrong, nor my tongue utter deceit. Far be it from me to that I should justify You; till I die I will not put away my integrity from me. I will hold fast to my innocence and will not let it go, my heart shall not reproach me as long as I live. May my enemy be like the wicked and my adversary like the unjust. For what is the hope of the hypocrite though he gained, when G-d takes away his soul. Will G-d hear his cry when trouble comes upon him? Does he delight in the Almighty and does he call upon G-d at all times? I will teach you about the hand of G-d; that which is (the way) with the Almighty I will not hide. Indeed, you yourselves have all seen. Why is it then that you deal in such vanities? This is the lot of a wicked man with G-d and the heritage which tyrants receive from the Almighty. If his children be multiplied it is for the sword; and his offspring will not be satisfied with bread. His survivors will be buried by (pestilence) death, and his widows will not weep.

Though he heap up silver like dust and prepare garments like the clay; He may prepare, but the righteous will wear it; and the innocent will divide the silver. He builds his house like a spider and like a booth that the watchman makes. He lies down rich, but will not be gathered (for burial). He opens his eyes and he is no more. Terrors overtake him like a flood, a storm snatches him away in the night. The east wind lifts him up and he is gone, and it hurls him out of his place. He will cast upon him without pity; out of his hand (his wealth) will surely escape. Men clench their fists at him and hiss him from his place.

COMMENTARY: CHAPTERS 26 and 27

Job makes the final reply to his three friends in a balanced and calculated brief, like an advocate's final argument in a courtroom. He begins with a sarcastic and biting remark. How inadequate was their comfort and how presumptuous for them to teach him about G-d.

The remainder of Chapter 26 consists of Job's lofty description of the greatness of G-d. He depicts several stages and several phases of creation. "He stretches out the north over empty spaces and suspends earth over nothingness." This sentence sounds like a poetic expression predicting future scientific discoveries that the earth is floating in space. The last sentence in this chapter "Behold these are but the outer edges of His ways; only a whisper of Him do we catch; who can perceive the thunder of His omnipotence." (14)

In Chapter 27 he begins by protesting to G-d regarding the bitterness of his lot. Nevertheless, he reaffirms his moral integrity. In spite of his own misery, he describes in detail the greater misery of "the sinner's portion from G-d." Job meditates on the doom and destruction of the wicked. Even though they may accumulate money, build houses and establish position, only to be crushed at the end.

Biblical critics seek to justify their criticism of the Bible. If, on the surface, the content of a speech does not appear "logical" to them, they make changes, transpose sentences, paragraphs and chapters from the accepted texts, to suit each their own interpretations.

In the case of these two chapters, we have the latest daring and presumptuous comment in the Anchor Bible, as follows: "Chapters 26 and 27 are thoroughly scrambled. A considerable part of Job's reply presents the viewpoint of the friends which Job all the while has denied and refuted. Some rearrangement is obviously necessary and it is possible to apportion the material in several ways to make reasonably consistent the continuation of the argument. Various rearrangements have been proposed. We submit that the simplest and most satisfactory expedient is to augment Bildad's abbreviated discourse in Chapter 25."

Many of these Bible critics break up Chapter 25 and 26 and assign these chapters to speakers of their choice. Chapter 28 is not in its place, they say! Chapter 28 is placed between Chapters 37 and 38.

In other words, these critics change the accepted Biblical text of Job's speeches. Just because Job is expressing the greatness and power of G-d seem contradictory to them. If only some of these non-Jewish and many Jewish scholars would heed the Talmudic comment on another Biblical book that contains contradictory thoughts.

"Rabbi Yehudah said in Rav's name: 'The sages wished to exclude the Book of Ecclesiastes from the Canon (Bible) because its words are self-contradictory. Yet why did they not hide it? Because its beginning is religious teaching and its end is religious teaching!" (Talmud Sabbath 30b)

In my introduction to this very book of *Ecclesiastes; Stories to Live By,* to which the above Talmudic comment makes reference, I challenge these Biblical critics with the following.

"This book expresses skepticism, pessimism and determinism as well as faith. These are the changing moods and the successive views of a thinking man, rather than simply disconnected ruminations. The underlying unity of thought and belief in the book, despite the apparently startling contradictions, is illustrated in this story."

"The sun and the moon met. The moon complained about its unfortunate lot in the world. "You the sun, you shine, you bring warmth and light to man. I shine in the night and even during the freezing winter nights." The sun reacted with sympathy and said: "Since you must serve in the severe frosty nights let us order a cloak for you, for the winter season." All the tailors in the world were summoned to fashion a cloak for the moon. None would accept the order. "How can we make a cloak for one whose shape and size is constantly changing? Sometimes the moon is small and thin, then it grows to half a circle, then it develops into a round, fat, full circle."

"Man too does not remain static. His thoughts and opinions change with his experience and knowledge."

The Biblical critics cannot accept Job's expression of the greatness of G-d and his detestation of the wicked. There are valid reasons for Job's thoughts. These are consistent with the faith he maintains throughout the book. He wants to prove to his friends that he did not need them to teach him this subject. Also, his vision may have expanded as a result of his suffering.

These two chapters express Job's depth of faith following the expression of his depth of complaints and rebellion.

Chapter 28

TEXT

There is a mine for silver and a place where they refine gold. Iron is taken out of the earth and copper is melted from rock. An end does he set to darkness and explores to the furthest bounds the ore from darkness and dense darkness. He breaks open a shaft far from the inhabited place forgotten of the foot (who walk overhead). They are suspended far from men, they swing to and fro. The earth, out of which comes bread, is under its surface turned up, as it were with fire. Its tones are the source of sapphires, and it has dust of gold. The path no bird of prey knows, nor has the vulture's eye seen it. The proud beasts have not trodden it, nor has the lion passed over it. He lays his hand upon the flinty rock. He overturns the mountains from the roots. He hews canals through the rocks, all precious things his eye sees. He binds the streams from trickling and what is hidden he brings to light.

But where can wisdom be found? And where is the place of understanding? Man knows not its value; nor is it found in the land of the living. The deep says, "It is not in me." Pure gold can not be given for it, nor can silver be weighed out as its price. It cannot be valued with the gold of Ophir, with precious onyx and sapphire. Gold and glass cannot equal it; nor can articles of fine gold be exchanged for it. No mention may be made of coral and crystal; the acquisition of wisdom is above rubies. The topaz of Ethiopia does not equal it, nor can it be valued with pure gold. From where, then, does wisdom come? And where is the place of understanding? It is hidden from the eyes of all the living and concealed from the birds of the heavens. Destruction and death say, "with our ears have we heard a report of it."

G-d understands its way and He knows its place. For He looks to the end of the earth and He sees under the whole heaven. When He made a weight for the wind, and meted out the waters by measure. When He made a law for the rain, and a way for the lighting of the thunder. Then did He see it and declare it. He established it and also searched it out. Then He said to man: Behold, the fear of the Lord, that is wisdom; and to depart from evil is understanding.

COMMENTARY

Job begins with a detailed description how man seeks hidden treasures of gold, silver, copper and precious stones. Man is successful in finding these by reason of his human wisdom. But Job realizes now, through his suffering and afflictions, that there is a superior wisdom, the divine knowledge that rules the world. The wisdom that contains the divine purpose in human struggle and human suffering—that man cannot find. Technological and scientific understanding was granted to man, but the divine wisdom that rules the universe is incomprehensible to him.

This reminds us of the episode of Adam and Eve in the Garden of Eden. "And the Lord G-d commanded the man saying: 'From every tree of the garden you are free to eat; but from the tree of the knowledge of good and evil you must not eat.'" (Genesis 2:16-17)

Like the first man, we may pursue and explore every aspect of nature, but the fruit of the tree of good and evil is forbidden to man.

117

Job concludes this chapter stating that divine wisdom G-d alone possesses. "Then He did see it and declared it. He established it and He searched it out. Then He said to man: 'Behold the fear of the Lord, that is wisdom: And to depart from evil, is understanding.' " (27-28)

"Fear of the Lord and to depart from evil" that is true wisdom. Technological knowledge can be distorted and become destructive of mankind, as we witnessed in our own day in Hitler Germany. There knowledge was misused to annihilate human beings. The following story is illustrative of the danger of wisdom without morality.

It is told of a Nazi officer who was interrogating a Jew. With the sadistic intention of frustrating the man in his clutches the Nazi said, "One eye of mine is artificial. It was set by the greatest German eye surgeon. No one can tell that there is a difference between my natural and the artificial eye. If you can tell which is the artificial eye I shall set you free." The tired, sick Jewish man lifted up his finger and pointed, "This is your glass eye." Enraged, the Nazi raved, "How did you know?" The answer was, "Your artificial eye is more human than your natural eye."

There is a succinct Biblical comment fittingly reflecting the limitations of human wisdom.

"He has made everything properly in its time; He also put eternity in their hearts but man can never comprehend the plan of G-d's work in its entirety." (Ecclesiastes 3:11) This sentence begins with a positive affirmation of divine rule. Although man may understand fragmentary parts of life and the universe, he is incapable of grasping "in its entirety" the purpose that underlies it all.

Chapters 29, 30 and 31

*And Job continued to take up his parable and said:
O, that I were as in the months of old, as the days when
G-d guarded me. When His lamp shone over my head, and
by His light I walked through darkness. As I was in the
ripeness of my days, when the confidence of G-d was upon
my tent. When the Almighty was still with me and when
my young ones were around me. When my steps were
washed with butter and the rock poured out for me streams
of oil. When I went out to the gate near the city, I prepared my seat in the open place. Young men saw me and
hid themselves, and the aged rose up and stood. Princes
stopped talking and placed their hands upon their mouths.
The voice of the nobles was hushed and their tongue
cleaved to their palate. For the ear that heard, called me
happy, and the eye that saw, testified for me. Because I delivered the poor who cried, and the orphan who had none
to help him. The blessing of him who was about to perish
came upon me, and I caused the heart of the widow to sing.
I put on righteousness and it clothed me, my justice was a
robe and mitre to me. Eyes was I to the blind and feet was*

119

I to the lame. I was a father to the needy and the cause of him I did not know, I searched out. And I broke the jaws of the wrongdoer and drew the prey out of its teeth. Then I said: 'I shall die with my nest, and I shall multiply my days as the phoenix. My root is spread out to the water and the dew will lodge on my boughs. My glory will ever be new with me, and my bow renewed in my hand. To me, men listened and waited and kept silence for my counsel. After my words, they did not speak again, and my speech dropped upon them (like raindrops). They waited for me as for the rain and opened their mouths as for the spring rain. I smiled on them when they had no confidence and the light of my countenance they never cast down. I chose their way and sat as chief, and dwelt like a king in the army as one who comforts mourners.

TEXT: CHAPTER 30

But now they who are younger than I, laugh at me, whose fathers I scorned to put with the dogs of my flock. Indeed, of what possible use can the strength of their hands be unto me over whom ripe age has perished? With want and famine, in solitude, they flee into the wilderness, in darkness, ruin, and desolation. Who pluck up mallows by the bushes and have broom-bush roots as their bread. They are driven from the midst (of men), who are shouted after, as after a thief. To dwell in the clefts of the valleys, in holes of the earth and rocks. Among the bushes they howl, under briars they huddle together, the children of the worthless and nameless who were outcasts from the land. And now I am become their song and I am a byword to them. They abhor me, they stay far from me, they do not refrain from spitting in my face. Because He has loosened my bowstrings and afflicted me, they have cast off restraint in my presence. On my right hand, they rise up in swarms, they push away my feet, and they level against me their ways of destruction. They break up my path, they help me in my downfall even though they have no one to aid them. As though a wide breach, they advance under the crash, they roll on. Terrors are turned upon me, they chase

120

my honor as the wind, and like a cloud my welfare has passed away. And now my soul is poured out within me; days of affliction have taken hold of me. The night pierces my bones from my body, and my sinews take no rest. By the great force (of the disease) is my garment disfigured, it enclosed me as the collar of my coat. He has cast me into the mire, and I am made like dust and ashes. I cry to You and You do not answer me, I stand up and You fixed Your regard against me. You have changed into one that is cruel to me, with the strength of Your hand You hate me. You lift me up to ride on the wind and dissolve in me all wise counsel. For I know You will bring me back to death and to the house appointed for all the living. Does not one in ruin stretch out his hand or does one not, in misfortune, cry for help? Did I not weep for him whose (time) day was hard, was not my soul grieved for the needy? But I hoped for good and evil came, and I waited for light, but darkness came. My inwards boil; days of affliction have come upon me. I go about blackened, but not by the sun, I arise in the assembly and cry for help. I have been a brother to jackals and a companion to ostriches. My skin has grown black upon me, and my bones burn from dryness. Therefore my harp has become mourning and my flute, into the voice of those who weep.

TEXT: CHAPTER 31

I have made a covenant with my eyes; how can I look (lustfully) upon a maiden? For what is the portion of G-d from above and the lot from the Almighty on high? Is it not calamity to the unrighteous and disaster to those who do wrong? Does He not see my conduct and count all my steps? If I have walked with falsehood and my foot has hastened to deceit, let me be weighed in just scales and may G-d know my integrity. If my step has strayed from the way and my heart followed my eyes, and if anything stained my hands, may I sow and another eat and may my crops be uprooted. If my heart has been enticed by a woman, and I have lain in wait at my neighbors door; then let my wife grind for another and others bend over her. For that is

121

licentiousness, a sin that calls for judgment. For it is a fire that devours to destruction and it would uproot all my increase. If I despised the claim of my male and female servants when they contended with me; what shall I do when G-d arises and when He examines, what shall I answer Him? Did not He who make me in the womb make him? And did not One fashion us in the womb? If I withheld what the poor desired or caused the eyes of the widow to fail; while I ate my food alone and the orphan shared none of it.

For, from my youth, he grew up with me as with a father, from infancy, I guided her! If I had seen any wandered without clothing, or the needy without a garment; If his loins did not bless me and he was not warmed with the fleece of my sheep. If I raised my hand against the orphan because I saw my advantage in the gate. Then let my shoulder-blade fall from my shoulder and my arm be broken from its socket. For calamity from G-d is a dread to me, and because of His Majesty, I was powerless. If I made gold my confidence and called fine gold my trust; If I rejoiced because my wealth was great and because my hand acquired much; If I beheld the sun when it shined or the moon moving in splendor; and my heart was secretly enticed and my hand has risen up to my mouth. This also is a sin that calls for judgment; for I should have been false to G-d above. If I have rejoiced at my enemies ruin or exulted when evil befell him? I did not permit my mouth to sin by calling down a curse upon his life. If the men of my tent did not say: "Is there anyone who has not been satisfied with his meat? The stranger did not lodge in the street, my doors I opened to the roadside. If after the manner of men I concealed my transgressions hiding my sin in my bosom. Because I dreaded the great crowds and the contempt of families terrified me, so that I kept silence and did not go out of doors. O, that I had someone to hear me, behold here is my signature, let the Almighty answer me and the scroll which my opponent has written. I would wear it on my shoulder; and like a crown bind it on me. The number of my steps I would declare. I would approach Him

122

like a prince. If my land cry out against me and its furrows weep together; If I ate its products without paying and brought its owners to despair, let thorns grow instead of wheat and foul weeds instead of barley. The words of Job are ended.

COMMENTARY: CHAPTERS 29, 30 and 31

In his concluding speech, Job makes a brilliant summary of his case. In Chapter 29 he depicts retrospectively his former honors and happiness. In Chapter 30 he describes in detail his present misery. In Chapter 31 he outlines the Biblical code of ethics he had lived by which justifies his claim of innocence and his hope for G-d's vindication.

This logical and legal brief forms a dramatic expression of his past, his present and his hope for the future. This parallels a Talmudic version of King Solomon's life which had three periods.

"Rav and Shmuel differed (about Solomon); one said that Solomon was first king and then a commoner. The other said he was first a king and then a commoner, and then a king again." In a mystifying manner, the Talmud further relates, "King Solomon was hurled away from his throne in Jerusalem. He (Solomon) used to go around begging and saying, wherever he went, 'I, Koheleth, was King over Israel in Jerusalem.'" (Talmud Gittin 68b)

King Solomon, deposed, from his royal position, degraded and deprived of his elementary needs, refused to give up hope for his restoration. Job in his concluding speech makes a superb summary of the three stages of his life. He describes his happy and revered position of the past. He draws a graphic picture of his present misery. But then, he outlines the ethical conduct of his life on which he bases his call that G-d justify him. Job, too, never gave up hope.

In Chapters 29 and 30, Job's reactions portray a normal human response to conditions of plenty and the opposite, conditions of adversity. The Psalmist speaks poetically of this contrast. "To declare Your kindness in the morning and Your faithfulness in the night" (Psalms 92:2). The application is made by our sages, that "in the morning" refers to a time when G-d showers blessings and goodness. At such time we readily declare "Your kindness." But "in the night" refers to a period when one suffers misery and misfortune. Then we can only declare "Your faithfulness."

A similar truth is expressed in the Bible (Psalms 36:7). "Your righteousness is like the high mountains and Your acts of justice like a great deep." In time of well-being and prosperity we see and accept G-d's righteousness because it is so obvious, without question "like the high mountains." In time of adversity and misfortune we can see no reason or justice for our misery, just as one cannot see anything in a deep empty pit.

In Chapter 31, Job reaffirms his faith. Job does not give up hope for his future. From the beginning to the end of the book, Job speaks explicitly and implicity about his faith in G-d. His steadfast faith is the source of his hopes. Had he given up, he could not have survived. The physical diseases, the social humiliation and the mental terror did not kill him because he had hope in G-d's response and vindication.

In a conversation between King Hezekiah and the prophet Isaiah, the King cuts short the prophet by saying "I have a tradition from my father's father that even if a sword is leveled at a man's throat, he should not give up hope."

This incident is related in the Talmud. The prophet Isaiah came to visit the sick King and told him, "command your household for you will die and not live. You will die in this world and not live in the world to come." The king asked: "Why such a severe sentence"? The prophet answered: "because you did not marry." The king replied "I did not marry because it was shown to me that I would have unfit children." The prophet answered: "Divine plans are not your concern. What is expected of you, you should have done and what is agreeable to G-d, let Him do."

The king offers to marry the prophet's daughter. Perhaps then, they would have good children. The prophet replies that it is too late, for his end had already been decreed. The king in short tense phrases said to the prophet, "Son of Amoz: end your prophecy and go. For I have received a tradition from my father's father that even if a sword is placed on a man's throat he must not give up hope for mercy."

An 11th Century Rabbi relates a story that once a rich, despondent man mistakenly judged a poor man as one who gave up all hope. The story tells that a very rich man became dejected and depressed. In this unhappy state, he was advised to spend his fortune on charity and doing good for people. This would bring him a purpose in life on earth and a reward in his future life. The rich man accepted the idea, but he vowed to help only those who have abandoned all hope as he himself had. He began a search for poor people. He found a poor man dressed in rags sitting on a dung heap. There, he thought, was a man who needs help. This man must have given up all hope. He seems tormented by need and waiting for death.

The rich man approached the poor man and handed him 100 gold pieces. The poor man opened his eyes in amazement and asked "Why do you give me so much money? Why have you selected me from among all the poor for this gift?"

The rich man replied: "I took a vow to give my money only to a man who had lost all hope in life, therefore I wanted to give my money to you." "Take back your gold" cried the poor man. "Only a fool or one who denies that there is a G-d in heaven can lose all hope in life." The rich man felt insulted and said: "Is this how you reward my compassion for you? How have I deserved your rebuke? The poor man answered: "You are under the mistaken impression that you have been good to me. It is just the opposite. You offered me your gold because you thought I am without hope. Only the dead are without hope."

Parables and Anectdotes

ON JOB

"Rovo said: 'Job sought to remove the guilt from the whole world. He said: "Sovereign of the Universe, you have created the ox with cloven hoofs and you have created the donkey with whole hoofs. You have created Paradise and you have created Gehinom (Hell). You have created righteous men and you have created wicked men and who can prevent your plan?" His companion answered him. "Indeed you are doing away with fear and diminishing devotion before G-d. (Job 15:4) If G-d created the evil inclination, He also created its spice." (its antidote—the Torah)

—Baba Bathra 16a

"G-d admonishes Job for his lack of patience saying, 'Why do you complain when suffering comes upon you? Do you consider yourself greater than Abraham, whom I tempted with many trials and he did not complain? Are you more worthy than Aaron to whom I showed greater honor than to any other human being for I sent the angels out of the Holy of Holies, when he entered the place? Yet when his two sons died, he did not murmur.' "

—Psikta Rabbati 191

"G-d said to Job: 'What do you prefer, poverty or suffering?' Job replied: 'Lord of the Universe, I am ready to accept all the troubles in the world, but not poverty, for if I go to the market place without a peruta (small coin) for buying, what shall I eat?' When suffering came upon him he began to complain against G-d's justice. Elihu said to him: 'Why do you complain? Did you not say that you preferred all kinds of suffering to poverty? Did you not yourself choose suffering?' "

—Midrash Rabba Genesis 31:12

"Rabba said: 'Job blasphemed with the mention of a tempest, and with a tempest he was answered. He blasphemed with mention of a tempest as Job said: He wracks me with a tempest and increases my wounds without cause (Job 9:17). Job asked G-d: Perhaps a tempest has passed before You and caused You to confuse "Iyov" (Job) and "Oyev" (enemy).

Job was answered through a tempest as it is written: "Then the Lord answered Job out of the whirlwind and said (Job 38:1) I have created many hairs on the body of man and for every hair I have created a separate pore, so that two should not grow from the same pore, for if two were to grow from the same groove, they would impair the sight of a man. I do not confuse one pore with another; and shall I then confuse (your name—Job) "Iyov" with (the word—enemy) "Oyev"?

'Who has divided a channel for the overflowing of water.' (Job 38:25) Many snowflakes have I created in the clouds, and for every one a separate mold, so that two snowflakes should not issue from the same mold, since if two drops issued from the same mold, they would wash away the soil, and it would not produce a fruit. I do not confuse one drop with another, and shall I confuse "Iyov" and "Oyev"?

"A path for the thunderbolt (Job 38:25). Many thunder-claps have I created in the clouds, and for each clap a separate path, so that two claps should not travel by the same path, since if two claps traveled by the same path, they would devastate the world. I do not confuse one thunder-clap with another, and shall I confuse "Iyov" with "Oyev"?

'Do you know the time when the mountain goats give birth'(Job 39:1). This mountain goat is cruel towards her young. When she crouches for delivery, she goes up to the top of a mountain so that the young shall fall down and be killed, and I prepare an eagle to catch it in his wings and set it before her, and if he were one second too soon or too late, it would be killed. I do not confuse one moment with another, and shall I confuse "Iyov" with "Oyev"?

'Do you watch the travail of the hinds? (Job 39:1) This hind has a narrow womb. When she crouches for delivery I prepare a serpent which bites her at the opening of the womb and she is delivered of her offspring; and were it one second too soon or too late, she would die. I do not confuse one moment with another and shall I confuse "Iyov" with "Oyev"?

—Baba Bathra 16a

"Job speaks without knowledge and his words are without insight." (Job 34:35) Rovo said: "This teaches that a man is not held responsible for what he says when in distress." (Job here is blamed for ignorance and not for wickedness.)

—Baba Bathra 16

RETRIBUTION

Hillel saw a skull floating on the river. (He recognized that this was the skull of a well-known robber.) Hillel said: "Because you drowned others, you were drowned; and at the end, those that drowned you shall themselves be drowned."

—Sukkah 53a

"But where indeed does the Torah say, 'Wickedness proceeds from the wicked?' It says implicitly in the verse 'But G-d deliver him into his hand.' For what is scripture speaking about here? About two men, one of whom killed a person with premeditation, and the other killed inadvertently, and in neither case were there witnesses to the deed, who could testify about it. Consequently, the former was not put to death and the latter was not forced into banishment to a city of refuge. Now G-d brings them together at the same inn. He, who killed with premeditation, happens to sit beneath a ladder, and the other, who killed inadvertently, ascends the ladder and falls (when descending it) upon the man who killed with premeditation, and kills him. Witnesses now being present they testify against him so compelling him to be banished to one of the cities of refuge. The result is that he who killed inadvertently is banished

128

and he who killed with premeditation actually suffers death."

—Rashi, Mishpatim, Makkos 2:1

"You shall not make other G-ds with me; gods of silver, or gods of gold you should not make unto you" (Exodus 20:20). "Do not behave towards Me as heathens behave towards their gods. When happiness comes to them they sing praises to their gods, but when retribution comes upon them they curse their gods. If I bring happiness upon you give thanks, but when I bring sufferings, also give thanks."

—Mechilta, Exodus 20

"Seven types of retribution come upon the world for seven capital transgressions. If some give the tithe and some do not, there comes a famine from drought. Then some suffer hunger while some have plenty. If (all) resolved not to give Tithes there comes a famine from tumult and drought. And if they will not set apart the dough-offering there comes an all consuming famine. Pestilence comes upon the world because of crimes deserving the death penalties enacted in the Torah that are not brought before the court and because (of the transgression of the laws of) the Seventh Year's produce. The sword comes upon the world because of the delaying of justice and the perverting of justice; and because of those who teach the Torah (law) not according to Halacha. Fierce beasts come upon a world because of idolatry and incest and bloodshed and because of not allowing the land to rest in the Sabbatical year."

—Avoth 5:11

"He (Rabbi Akiva) used to say: All is given on a pledge and the net is cast over all living (no one can escape Divine justice). The shop stands open and the shop-keeper (G-d) gives credit and the account book lies open and the hand writes: Everyone who wishes to borrow let him come and borrow. And the collectors go their round continuously every day and exact payment from men with their consent or without their consent, for they have that on which they can rely; and the judgment is a judgment of truth; and all is made ready for the banquet." (the reward for the righteous).

—Avoth 3:20

"Rabbi Jacob said: This world is like a vestibule before the world to come. Prepare yourself in the vestibule that you may enter the banquet hall."

—Avoth 4:21

"He (Rabbi Eliezer Hakappor) used to say: They who have been born (are destined) to die, and the dead (are destined) to be made alive, and they who live (are destined after death) to be judged, that men may know, and to proclaim and understand that He is G-d, He is the Maker, He is the Creator, He is the Discerner, He is the Judge, He is the Witness, He is the Complainant; and it is He who shall judge. Blessed be He in whose presence is neither wrongdoing nor forgetfulness nor partiality nor taking of bribes. And know that every thing is according to the reckoning. And let not your (evil) nature promise you that the grave will be your refuge; for despite yourself were you fashioned and despite yourself were you born, and despite yourself you die, and despite yourself you shall hereafter give account and reckoning before the King of Kings the Holy One, blessed be He."

—Avoth 4:29

"Shall not the Judge of all the earth do justly?" (Genesis 8:25) Rabbi Levi said: If it is the world You seek, there can be no justice; and if it is justice (without mercy) You seek, there can be no world. Why do You grasp the rope by both ends? You want both the world and justice.

130

Choose one of them. For if You do not relent a little the world cannot endure."

—Midrash Rabba Genesis 39:6

Rabbi Isaac said: "Man is judged only by his deeds at the time of judgment, as it is said (of Ishmael) 'For G-d heard the voice of the lad as he is there.' " (Genesis 21:17)

—Rosh Hashana 16:b

LONG-SUFFERING

"There were ten generations from Adam to Noah, to show how great was His long-suffering, for all the generations continually provoked Him until He brought upon them the waters of the flood. There were ten generations from Noah to Abraham, to show how great was His long-suffering for all the generations continually provoked Him, until our father Abraham came and received the reward of them all.'

—Avoth 5:2

"And it shall be very tempestuous round about him." (Psalms 50:3) Which teaches that G-d is particular with those round about Him, (the pious) even for matters as light as a single hair. Rabbi Nechemia derived the same lesson from the verse: 'G-d is greatly to be feared in the assembly of the saints and is in reverence of all of them that are about Him." (Psalms 89:8) Rabbi Chanina said: "If a man says that G-d is lax in the execution of justice, his life shall be forfeited, for it is stated 'He is the rock, His work is perfect; for all His ways are judgment.' (Deuteronomy 32:4) But Rabbi Chono, or as others reported, Rabbi Samuel ben Nachmani, said: 'Why is it written 'long-suffering' (Exodus 34:6 plural) and not long-suffering (singular). It must indicate long-suffering to both the righteous (who don't have total reward in this world) and

131

the wicked (who don't have total punishment in this world)."

—Baba Kamma 50b

"What is the meaning of 'slow to anger' as ascribed to G-d? It indicates keeping anger far away. The matter may be likened to a King who had two legions consisting of cruel soldiers. He said: 'If they dwell in the same city with me, should the inhabitants provoke me, my men will stand against them and act cruelly towards them. I will therefore send the soldiers on a long journey so that if the citizens provoke me, before I bring my soldiers back, they will seek to appease me and I will accept it of them.' Similarly, G-d said "Aph and Chaimo are the angels of destruction. I will send them a long way off so that if the children of Israel provoke Me, before I can fetch the angels back, the people will repent and I will accept it of them.' "

—Yerushalmi Taanith 65b

FREE WILL
"He (Akiva) used to say: 'Everything is foreseen (by G-d) and everything is revealed, yet all is in accordance with the will of man.' "

—Avoth D'Reb Nathan 39

"The name of the angel appointed over conception is 'Night.' He takes the seed and places it before G-d and says, 'Master of the Universe, what is this to be, mighty or weak, wise or foolish, rich or poor?' But he does not say wicked or righteous. For Rabbi Chanina said, 'All is in the hands of heaven, except the fear of heaven.' "

—Niddah 16b

"The Holy One, blessed be He, who is called righteous and upright, created man in His image only that he be righteous and upright like Him. And why did He create

132

the Yetzer hora (evil inclination)? Since it is written of man: 'For the imagination of man's heart is evil from his youth (Genesis 8:21). Now that it says he is evil, who can make him (man) good? The Holy One, blessed be He, says: 'It is you who make yourself evil. Why? A child of five, six, seven, eight or nine does not sin; but from the age of ten he develops an evil impulse.' "

—Midrash Tanchuma Genesis 7

"Behold I set before you this day a blessing and a curse (Deuteronomy 11:26) Why is this stated? Since it has likewise been said, 'See, I have set before you this day life and good; death and evil' (Deuteronomy 30:19). Perhaps the Israelites will say, 'Since G-d has set before us two ways, the way of life and the way of death, we can walk in whichever way we like. Therefore it is taught, "Choose life, that you may live, you and your seed' " (Deuteronomy 30:19).

A parable of a person who was sitting at the cross roads—before whom two paths branched out. The beginning of one path was clear, but its end was full of thorns. The second path was thorny at the start, but the latter part was clear. He used to warn the travellers and say to them, 'You see this path whose beginning is clear, and for two or three steps you walk in comfort, but at the end you meet with thorns. Now you see the other path. The beginning is thorny, for two or three steps you walk through thorns, but in the end, you come to a straight road.' Similarly, Moses said to Israel: 'You see the wicked prospering, but in the end they are discarded. You also see the righteous in trouble. For two or three days they suffer in this world, but in the end they will be rejoicing.' "

—Sifre Deuteronomy on 11:26

PART III

ELIHU SPEAKS

Introductory Note

Elihu finds Job's three friends deficient in the debate and unable to defend G-d's justice. He is equally angry with Job. Elihu discards the friends' contention, that suffering is always punishment for sins. Elihu is also displeased with Job's complaint that he is suffering without cause, and therefore, G-d is unjust.

Elihu presents, with great clarity, the doctrine that suffering often comes to the upright, as a warning. If the warning goes unheeded, suffering comes as a discipline, to prevent the righteous from sinning.

Elihu concludes by pointing out G-d's providence in nature. He depicts G-d not only great in power, but true and just. It behooves Job, therefore, to repent.

Elihu ends his long speech with these words: "The Almighty, whom we cannot find out, is excellent in power and judgment, great in justice. He does no violence. Men should therefore, fear Him; He regards not those who are wise in heart."

Chapters 32 and 33

TEXT: CHAPTER 32

So these three men ceased answering Job because he was righteous in his own eyes. Then Elihu, the son of Barachel, the Buzite, of the family of Ram, became angry. He was angry with Job for considering himself more righteous than G-d. He was also angry with his three friends because they had found no answer, and yet had condemned Job, for they were older than he. Now, when Elihu saw that these three men had no answer, he became very angry. And Elihu, the son of Barachel, the Buzite replied and said: "I am young and you are very old; therefore I was afraid and dared not declare you mine opinion. I thought, age should speak and the mature in years should teach wisdom. However, it is the spirit in a man and the breath of the Almighty that gives him understanding. It is not the great (in age) that are wiser nor the elders who understand justice. Therefore I say 'listen to me. I, too, will declare my opinion.' Behold I waited while you spoke. I listened to your reasoning while you searched for words. I paid attention to you and, behold, there was no one to refute Job, none of you answered his words. Lest you say we have found a wise plan, let G-d reprove him not man. For he has not directed his words against me; and with your arguments, I will not answer him. They are dismayed, they answer no more; words have failed them. And am I to wait, because they ceased speaking for they stand still with no further answer. I, too, will answer my part; I, too, will state my opinion. For I am full of words, the spirit within me compels me. Behold, my bosom is like wine that has no vent, like new wine skins ready to burst. I will speak that I may get relief, I will open my lips and answer. I will not be partial toward anybody nor flatter any man. For I do not know how to flatter; else would my Maker soon take me away.

TEXT: CHAPTER 33

But now, hear my speech, O Job, and listen to all my words. Behold now I have opened my mouth, the tongue in my palate has spoken. My words reveal the uprightness of my heart and what my lips know they shall speak sincerely. The spirit of G-d has made me, draw up before me, take your stand. Behold, in the sight of G-d I am like you. I, too, was formed out of clay. Behold, dread of me will not terrify you, nor will my pressure be heavy upon you. Surely you have spoken in my hearing and I heard the sound of the words. I am clean without transgression, I am innocent and without guilt. "Behold, He finds pretexts against me, He counts me as His enemy. He puts my feet in the stocks and watches all my paths." But in this you are not right, I will answer you; that G-d is mightier than man. Why do you strive against Him; For He does not answer in the manner of his (man's) words. For G-d speaks through one means and then another and (man) does not perceive it. In a dream, in a vision of the night, when deep sleep falls upon men in slumbers, upon the bed. He opens the ears of men and as a warning, He chastises them. To deter man from his deeds and rid man from his pride. To spare his soul from the pit and his life from perishing by the sword. And he is chastened with pain upon his bed and with ceaseless agony in his bones. So that his life abhors bread

and his appetite (abhors) the daintiest food. His flesh
wastes away so that it can not be seen and his bones that
protrude are unsightly. And so, he himself draws near to
the grave and his life, to the emissaries of death. If there be
with him an angel, an interpreter, one of a thousand to
vouch for man's uprightness. Then He is gracious to him
and says, "Deliver him from going down to the grave, I
have found a ransom." His flesh is tenderer than a child's;
he shall return to the days of his youth. He prays to G-d
and He accepts him. He sees His face with joy; and He re-
stores to man his integrity. He goes before men and says;
"I have sinned and perverted the right and it did not profit
me." He redeemed him from going into the pit so that he
may behold the light of life.

Behold, all these things does G-d do, twice—yes, three
times—with a man, to bring back his soul from the pit,
that he may be enlightened with the light of the living.

Give heed, O Job, listen to me. Be silent and let me
speak. Then if you have anything to say, answer me; speak,
for I desire to justify you. If not, you listen to me; be silent
and I will teach you wisdom.

COMMENTARY: CHAPTERS 32 AND 33

The dialogue between Job and his three friends ended.
Now, Elihu, a young and dynamic bystander is introduced.
He is incensed against both sides. He is angry at Job for
trying to justify himself by accusing G-d of injustice, and
against the three friends for their inadequate replies to Job.

In the prologue to this volume, the author presents a
concept that suffering is a test and trial of faith. The three
friends insist that suffering is a punishment for sin. Job,
who feels innocent of sin seeks an answer from G-d.
Elihu adds a new dimension, although it is not the total
answer to Job's question.

A very interesting and novel idea is presented in *Movo
L'sefer Eyov* by Yehudah Zlotnick. He translates two sentences in Elihu's speech to imply the concept of transmigra-
tion of souls. Elihu, thus, solves the problem of the suffer-

ing of the upright. Suffering may be due to the wrong committed in a previous existence.

In chapter 33:29-30 the usual translation reads: "Lo, all these things does G-d work, twice, even three times with a man, to bring back his soul from the pit, that he may be enlightened with the light of the living." Zlotnick translates these sentences: "Behold this G-d does. Two or three times with a man does he restore his soul from death to shine in the light of life." The author says he bases this view upon the opinion of the Ramban (Nachmanides) quoted by his disciple Bachya in his book *Kad Hakemach*.

Maimonides views Elihu's speech as new and indispensible to the book. "The new idea, which is peculiar to Elihu and has not been mentioned by the others, is contained in his metaphor of the angel's intercession. It is a frequent occurrence, he says, that a man becomes ill, approaches the gates of death and is already given up by his neighbors. If, then, an angel of any kind intercedes on his behalf and prays for him, the intercession and prayers are accepted. The patient rises from his illness, is saved, and returns to good health." (Maimonides, *Guide to the Perplexed,* Volume 3, Chapter 23)

Elihu answers Job more directly and realistically. G-d is neither silent nor indifferent. G-d speaks to us in two ways, in dreams as a warning for correction, or through suffering. Since a verbal warning is often unheeded, suffering comes to man to save him from his own self will and self destruction. Elihu is very emphatic. He declares: "For G-d speaks through one means and then another, though one does not perceive it. In a dream, in a vision of the night, when deep sleep falls upon men, in slumber upon the bed, He opens the ears of men and as a warning chastises them." (Job 33:14)

The Midrash speaks about warnings as a form of discipline, before punishment. "Behold I set before you this day a blessing and a curse." (Deuteronomy 11:26) The Midrash comments, "As it is written: 'He openeth their eyes to discipline and commands them to turn from iniquity. If they obey and serve, they shall spend their days in prosperity and their years in pleasantness. If they do not obey they will perish by the sword." (Job 36:10)

" 'He opens their ear to discipline' means: 'that G-d does not bring punishment to a person unless He first opens his ear to discipline and warns him to repent. If the individual returns to the right path, it is well with him. If not, He causes evil to this man. We learn this from Pharoah, King of Egypt. Before G-d brought a plague upon him, He sent a messenger, Moses, to warn him; as it says, 'If you refuse to let my people go, behold, tomorrow I will bring locusts into your border.' (Exodus 10:4) 'You exalt yourself against My people, that you will not let them go. Behold, tomorrow, about this time, I will cause it to rain a very grievous hail such as has not been in Egypt since the day it was founded even until now.' (Exodus 9:17,18) He warns man as a discipline." (Midrash Tanchuma on Deuteronomy 11:26)

The story is told about a man who had a mystifying and frightening dream. The angel of death appears and tells him: "Your time is up. I have come to take your life." The man is stunned and shocked and pleads for time. He protests such a sudden and fatal verdict without any warning. The man cries: "I am in the midst of several projects for my family and my business. It is a bit unfair to leave so unprepared and so unexpectedly."

His plea is accepted. The angel of death leaves him with a promise that he will not return for his fatal mission without an advance warning.

Ten years later the stern angel reappeared and announced, "Now your time is up. This time it is final." In anger the man cried out, "But you promised you will not come without advance warning." "I kept my promise" came the firm reply, "but you paid no attention to all my warnings. Do you remember when you were involved in a head on collision on the highway? Your car was turned over and you walked away unhurt? Do you remember at a banquet in your honor and you blacked out suddenly and passed out? Can I help it if you did not take my warnings seriously?"

Chapter 34

Then Elihu replied and said: Hear my words, you wise men; give ear to me, O men of knowledge. For the ear tests words as the palate tastes food. Let us choose for us what is right, let us determine between our-selves what is good. For Job has said: "I am innocent and G-d has taken away my right. Though, I am right, I am accounted a liar; my wound has no cure though I am without fault." What man is there like Job? He drinks up scorn like water, who keeps company with evil doers and walks with wicked men. For he has said: It does a man no good to be in favor with G-d. Therefore hear me, O men of understanding, far be it from G-d to do evil and from the Almighty to do wrong. For the work of a man He renders to him, and grants every man according to his ways. Surely G-d will not act wickedly, neither will the Almighty pervert justice. Who entrusted the earth to Him and gave Him charge over the whole world? If He set His heart upon him (man) if He gathered to Himself his spirit and his breath, all flesh would expire at once and man return to the dust. Therefore, observe and hear this, listen to the voice of my words. Can one who hates justice rule? And will you declare guilty, Him, who is just and strong? Does one say to a King, "You are vile" or to nobles "you are wicked?" He shows no partiality to princes, nor favors the rich over the poor for they are all the work of His hands. In a moment they die, at midnight, the people are shaken and pass away, and the mighty are removed by an unseen hand. For His eyes are on man's conduct and He sees all his steps. There is no darkness nor great darkness where the evil doers may hide themselves. For He does not further impose upon man a time when to appear before G-d in judgment. He shatters mighty men without searching and sets up others in their place. Indeed, He knows their deeds, and overturns them in the night, and they are crushed. He strikes them as they are wicked in sight of all. Because they turned away from Him and had no regard for any of His ways, to bring to Him the cry of the poor and He hears the cry of the afflicted. When He grants peace who can condemn? If He hides His face who can see Him?—Be it upon a nation or man alike. When a hypocrite rules it is because of the sins of the people. For has any one said to G-d "I have borne my chastisement I will not offend." You teach me what I do not see; If I have done wrong, I will do it no more. Shall He make retribution as you wish? Since you reject it, now you must choose, not I: What you know, declare. Reasonable men will say to me and a wise man who listens to me, Job speaks without knowledge and his words are without insight. Would that Job may be tried to the end, because of his answering like wicked men. For he adds to his sin, he increases transgression among us, as he multiplies his words against G-d.

COMMENTARY

Maimonides describes Elihu's speech as "a profound and wonderful discourse."

In this chapter, Elihu answers Job's complaint that "Lo, I go forward but He is not there, and backward, but I can not perceive Him. On the left hand He is concealed and I can not behold Him; He wraps Himself on the right that I can not see Him." (23:8-9)

Elihu answered: "For His eyes are on man's conduct and He sees all his steps." (21) Elihu further makes the point in detail, that there is nothing hidden from G-d.

Elihu, however, introduces a concept of G-d hiding His face under certain circumstances. This idea is explicitly expressed in writing from Moses to Micha. Elihu says, "If He keep quiet, who can condemn, and if He hides His face who can see Him?" (29)

Before the death of Moses, G-d told him that in the event the people will break His covenant with Him: "And I will surely hide My face in that day because of all the evil that they have done in turning to other gods." (Deuteronomy 31:18) "And He said: I will hide My face from them, I will see what their end shall be." (Deuteronomy 32:20)

The Psalmist cries: "You did hide Your face, I was frightened." (Psalms 30:8) "Truly You are a G-d who hides Yourself, G-d of Israel, the Savior." (Isaiah) "And for whose manifold wickedness I have hid My face from this city." (Jeremiah 35:5)

"Then shall they cry unto the Lord and He will not answer them; but He will hide His face from them at that time, inasmuch as they have done wicked deeds." (Micha 3:4) "The nations shall know that the house of Israel went into exile for their iniquity because they broke faith with Me. And I hid My face from them according to their uncleanliness and according to their transgressions, I did it unto them and I hid My face from them."

"Therefore thus says the Lord G-d: 'Now I will bring back the captivity of Jacob and have compassion upon the whole House of Israel and I will vindicate My holy name. . . . neither will I hide My face any more from them.'" (Ezekiel 39:23-29)

Isaiah and Ezekiel bring a message of hope that G-d will restore and save Israel. All the above quotations have one thing in common. These prophets are not talking about a hidden G-d, but a hiding G-d. The obvious implication is that man's evil conduct drives the Divine spirit away from man.

The Rabbis speak of the fact that originally the Divine

Presence was to dwell on earth. Gradually man's misconduct and corruption drove the Divine Presence back to heaven. Before the destruction of the Temple, says Rabbi Judah, in the name of Rabbi Yochanan, "The Divine Presence left Israel by ten stages." (Talmud Rosh Hashona 31a) The Midrash tells that the Shechina, the Divine Presence, was on earth, "But when Adam sinned, the Shechina withdrew and ascended to the first heaven. Cain sinned and the Shechina withdrew and ascended to the second heaven. In the generation of Enosh it went to the third; at the generation of the flood to the fourth; at the generation of the Tower of Babel to the fifth; at the time of the Sodomites to the sixth; and the time of the Egyptians to the seventh." (Midrash Rabbah 19)

"When the people of the world are righteous and observe the commands of the Torah, the earth becomes invigorated and fullness of joy prevails, because the Divine Presence rests upon the earth and there is gladness above and below. But when mankind corrupts its way and does not observe the commands of the Torah and sins before their Master, they as it were, drive the Divine Presence out of the world and the earth is left in a corrupt state." (Zohar-Genesis-Noah)

Some philosophers will speak of the hiding face of G-d as an eclipse, a period of time when such an obscuring occurs. We know that when an eclipse of the sun occurs the blocking out is not in the sun, but in our vision. In the same way, we may speak of the hiding face of G-d as an eclipse.

There is a Rabbinic story that the grandson of Rabbi Boruch was playing hide and seek with his friend. He hid himself and remained in his hiding place for a long time, waiting for his friend to look for him. Then he went out and saw that his friend was gone, apparently not having looked for him at all. He ran into the house crying and complaining about his friend. On hearing of this incident, Rabbi Baruch began to cry and said: "G-d too says: 'I hide, but there is no one to look for Me.' "

Chapter 35

TEXT

Then Elihu replied saying: Do you consider this to be right? You say: "I am more righteous than G-d? For you say: 'What advantage is it for you, what do I gain more than if I had sinned?' I will answer you and your friends with you. Look to the heavens and see, observe the skies above you. If you have sinned, how does it affect Him? And if your offenses be many, what do you do to Him? If you are righteous, what do you give Him? Or what benefit does He take from your hand? Your wickedness affects a man like yourself and your righteousness a fellow human being. Because of the multitude of oppressions they cry out; they call for help because of the power of the mighty. And nobody had said: 'Where is G-d my Maker who gives songs in the night, who teaches us more than the beasts of the earth and makes us wiser than the birds of heaven? There they cry out He does not answer because of the pride of evil men. Surely it is false that G-d does not hear and that the Almighty does not regard it. Although you say that you do not see Him, judgment is before Him and waits for Him. Even now, when there is none (of man's justice), he visits His anger but does not greatly regard sin. Yet Job opens his mouth in vanity; he multiplies words without knowledge.

COMMENTARY

Elihu, consistent with his basic approach that G-d teaches man through dreams and suffering, now gives special expression to a specific blessing G-d granted man. G-d created man with a higher intelligence. Elihu says: "Who teaches us more than the beasts of the earth and makes us wiser than the birds of heaven." (35:11) Indeed man's superiority over all living creatures is his gift of reason. Man is physically weaker and less equipped to fight than the animal. It takes man longer to achieve physical self reliance.

Fish and birds must become independent right after birth. Domestic animals achieve self reliance days after birth. The human child remains helpless for a long time. He must receive food, care, and be cleansed since he can not move in infancy.

Reason compensates man for his physical weakness. Man developed weapons that out-do the teeth, the fangs, the strength and the speed of the animals about him.

One of our great philosophers, Gersonides, ascribed to reason a position that controls and decides the fate of man. From Gersonides' lengthy comments on Elihu's speech we gather the essence of his philosophy.

Gersonides states that Elihu believes G-d has endowed all animals with certain organs by means of which they are preserved. Man was enriched with reason, that he could save himself from the evils of nature. The more man uses his reason, the more he will earn special Providence.

As for the apparent injustice in the world that Job sees, Elihu declares that nature and the natural laws as established by G-d have been intended for good. It is therefore no injustice if the wicked are also the recipients of the good. On the other hand, the evil befalling the righteous comes when they are lax in their ways. Then G-d removes His special Providence from them. Moreso, when evil comes to the righteous, it serves as a reminder to them that they began to turn away from the way of G-d. (36:10-11)

A way of redemption is offered to the righteous, to turn back to G-d. Then they will again be placed under special Providence. The wicked, not having special Providence, will not escape their evil end and eventually will become completely crushed. He concludes with a more spiritual solution. He proposes that the real good is, after all, the eternal good, the happiness of the soul. Whereas, the real evil, is the loss of such happiness. Then the result of good and evil, as we are able to see it, is only relative. What is important, is that the righteous have a way of redemption by means of their reason, and the wicked are deprived of this path, and its capacity to lead them to redemption. Reasonable man ought to accept correction and admonition which leads to a better life.

Rabbi Eliezer Ben Azariah holds that life is so sacred and significant, that man ought to be warned about the impediments of life as a physician warns a patient. Surely a doctor has no ulterior motives. The doctor has one single goal, to save the life of his patient and to heal his illness.

The repetition of warnings in the Bible causes Rabbi Eliezer to compare it to the warning a physician offers to his patient and he illustrates this idea with the following parable. "It may be compared to the case of a sick person visited by his physician. He (the doctor) said to him, 'Do not eat cold food, nor sleep in a damp place.' Another physician came and said to him, 'Do not eat cold food, nor sleep in a damp place so that you may not die!' A third physician came and said to him, 'Do not eat cold food, nor sleep in a damp place so that you may not die as Mr. So and So died!' " (Safro Leviticas 16:2) There we have three physicians. All make the same prognosis. All give the same prescription, but they speak differently. The first doctor only prescribes the remedy. The second physician adds a fatal warning. The third physician ceases to be theoretic. He supports his warning by relating a tragic experience that befell the patient's friend who ignored the doctor's warning.

Elihu adds one sound point. Instead of people "crying" when suffering comes, they ought to accept the warnings of admonition given to them by G-d, "G-d my Maker who gives songs in the night."

149

Chapters 36 and 37

TEXT: CHAPTER 36

Then Elihu continued and said: Bear with me a little and I will show you that there is more to be said on G-d's behalf. I will bring my knowledge from afar, and will ascribe righteousness to my Maker. For indeed my words are not false; one upright in mind is with you. Behold G-d is mighty and does not despise; mighty in strength and understanding. He preserves not the life of the wicked and grants justice to the poor. He does not withdraw His eyes from the righteous; He sets them with kings on the throne for ever and they are exalted. And if they be bound in chains and be caught in cords of affliction, then He makes known to them their deeds and their sins that they have acted arrogantly. He opens their ear to discipline and commands them to turn from iniquity. If they obey and serve, they shall spend their days in prosperity and their years in pleasantness! If they do not obey, they will perish by the sword and they will expire for the lack of knowledge. The hypocrites in heart harbor anger, they do not cry for help when He chastises them. Their souls die in youth and their lives end in shame. He delivers the afflicted by His affliction and opens their ear by tribulation. Furthermore, He removed you from distress into a broad place of unlimited room, and that which is set on your table is full of fatness. And you are full of the judgment of the wicked, justice and judgment will take hold. Beware, there is wrath, lest you be led away by abundance; nor let much ransom lead you astray. Will your wealth, that is without limit, avail, or all resources of your might? Do not long for the night when people are cut off in their place. Be careful that you do not run to evil for you clearly prefer this to submission. Behold, G-d is sublime in His power; who is a teacher like Him? Who can prescribe for Him His conduct? Who can say you have done wrong? Remember to magnify His work, which men behold. All men have looked upon it, though man can see it only from afar. Behold G-d is great beyond our knowledge; the sum of His years beyond comprehension. For He draws up the drops of water and it is distilled from His mist, which the clouds pour down and shower upon the multitudes of men. Also, can anyone understand the spreading of the clouds, the thundering from His pavilion? Behold, He spreads His light over it and covers the depths of the sea. For by these He judges the nations and provides food in abundance. He covers His hands with lightning which He commands toward a target. The thunder proclaims His presence and the storm His rousing anger.

TEXT: CHAPTER 37

At this also my heart trembles and leaps from its place. Listen closely to the roar of his voice, and the rumbling that goes out from His mouth. He flashes it beneath the whole heaven and His lightning to the ends of the earth. After it a sound roars; He thunders with His majestic voice; He does not restrain (the lightning) when His voice is heard. G-d thunders with His wondrous voice doing great things we cannot comprehend! For to the snow he says: "Fall to the earth!" Likewise to the downpour of rain and to the mighty bursts of rain. He seals up (suspends) the hand of every man that all men may know His work. Then the beast enters the lair and dwells in his den. From the cham-

ber comes the whirlwind and the cold from scattering winds. By the breath of G-d ice is formed and the broad waters are congealed. Also with moisture He loads the clouds and the cloud scatters His lightning. And it is turned round about by His guidance that they may do all He commands them, on the face of the inhabited world. He causes it to come, whether for discipline or for His land, or for mercy. Listen to this, O Job; stop and observe the wonders of G-d. Do you know how G-d lays His command upon them, how He causes the lightning flash from His clouds. Do you know the balancing of the clouds the wonders of One perfect in knowledge? Your garments are hot when the earth is still, because of the south wind. Can you spread out the sky with Him, strong as a molten mirror? Teach us what we shall say to Him; we cannot draw up a statement because of darkness (ignorance). Shall it be told that I would speak? Or if a man speaks will he be destroyed? As it is, men cannot gaze on the light (sun) when it is bright in the skies; but the wind has passed and cleared them. From the North comes golden splendour, around G-d is awesome majesty. The Almighty, whom we cannot find out, is excellent in power and judgment, great in justice, He does no violence. Men should therefore fear Him; He regards not those who are wise in heart.

COMMENTARY: CHAPTERS 36 and 37

Elihu concludes his speech on a note of consolation rather than critical rebuke. In addition, Elihu concentrates on the problems directly affecting Job. Elihu dismisses the complaint "why the wicked prosper" with the statement: "He preserves not the life of the wicked." However, the problem of the troublesome personal agony of Job "why the righteous suffer," Elihu spells out in more detail. He presents a reason for such occurrence. There is reason and design in G-d's affliction of the righteous. Elihu says: "He delivers the afflicted by His affliction and opens their ear by tribulation." (Job 36:15) What is the purpose for the suffering of the righteous? "He opens their ear to discipline."

(36:10) "Behold G-d is sublime in His power; who is a teacher like Him?" (36:22)

In Chapter 37, we detect a hint of what will follow in G-d's answer from the whirlwind. Elihu wants to convey to Job the grandeur of nature as the revelation of G-d's majesty, His power and His providence.

Then Elihu directs to Job questions concerning the processes by which G-d governs the natural phenomena and the universe. Since Job cannot answer how G-d rules the physical world, how can he presume to grasp the Divine knowledge of G-d's rule in the life of man?

Elihu's last phrase asks Job not to judge G-d; that no man is in a position either to comprehend nor to judge G-d. "Man should therefore fear Him; He regards not those who are wise in heart." (37:24)—those who presume to be wise in their own understanding.

Parables and Anecdotes

TO SUFFER

G-d gave Israel three precious gifts and all of them were given only through suffering. They are: the Torah, the Land of Israel, and the World to come.

—Brochoth 5a

Rova said, and some say Rabbi Chisda; "If a man sees suffering coming upon him, let him examine his conduct, as it is said, 'Let us search and try our ways and return to the Lord.' (Lamentation 3:40) If he has searched his deeds and found nothing, let him ascribe it to the neglect of the study of Torah. As it is said: 'Happy is the man whom You chastise, O Lord, and teach out of your Torah.' (Psalms 94:12) And if he attributed it to the above and found nothing, surely they are chastisements of love. As it is said: 'For whom the Lord loves he corrects.'" (Proverbs 3:12)

—Brochoth 5a

"Let a man rejoice in sufferings more than in happiness. For if a man has lived all his life in happiness, any sin which he may have committed has not been pardoned; but what is pardoned through suffering is forgiven him. Beloved is suffering, because just as the sacrifices secured acceptance, so does suffering secure acceptance. Nay, sufferings bring even greater acceptance, since sacrifices entail money only, while sufferings affect the body."

—Sifre Deuteronomy 32:73

Rabbi Huna said: " 'Behold it was very good' (Genesis), refers to the dispensation of happiness, 'and behold it was very good' to the dispensation of suffering." Can then suffering actually be very good? It is in fact so, because, through its instrumentality, men attain to the life of the future world. And so Solomon said: 'And reproofs of chastisements are the way of life.' (Proverbs 6:23) Say now, go out and see which road leads man to the life of the future world? Surely it is suffering."

—Midrash Rabba Genesis 9:10

TO FORGIVE

"It was taught, Rabbi Yossi ben Yehuda said: 'If a man commits a transgression, the first, second, and third time he is forgiven. The fourth time he is not forgiven, as it is said: "Thus says the Lord: For three transgressions of Israel, yea for four, I will not reverse it. " (Amos 2:6) And furthermore it says; Lo Behold, all these things does G-d do, twice, yea three times with a man. (Job 33:29) Why the second verse? One might have assumed that this applies only to a community, but not to an individual, therefore, 'Come and hear. Behold all these things does G-d do twice, yea three times with a man.' "

—Yoma 86b

Our Rabbis taught: If one falls sick and his life is in danger, he is told "make your confession," for all who are

154

sentenced to death make a confession. When a man goes out into the street, let him imagine that he is put into the hand of an officer. When he has a headache, let him imagine that he is put in irons, when he goes to bed (in illness) let him imagine that he ascended the scaffold to be punished. For whoever ascends the scaffold to be punished, if he has great advocates, he is saved, but if not, he is not saved. And these are a man's advocates: Repentance and good deeds. And even if nine hundred and ninety-nine argued for his guilt, while one argues in his favor, for it is said, "If there be with him an angel, an advocate, one among a thousand, to show to man what is right for him. Then He is gracious to him and says, 'Deliver him from going down to the pit.' " Rabbi Eliezer the son of Yossi Haglili said, "Even if nine hundred and ninety-nine reasons of that angel are in his disfavor, and one part is in his favor, he is saved, for it is said: 'An advocate, one (part) in a thousand.' "

—Sabbath 32

Rabbi Eliezer ben Jacob said: "He who performs one precept gains for himself one advocate, but he who commits one transgression acquires for himself one accuser. Repentance and good deeds are a shield against punishment."

—Avoth 4:13

"Even for the sake of a single righteous man does the world endure, as it says: 'But the righteous is the foundation of the world.' " (Proverbs 10:25)

—Yoma 38b

G-d said: "When I am the victor, I am the loser, and when I am defeated, I gain. I defeated the generation of the flood, did I not really lose, for I destroyed my world, as it is written! 'And He blotted out every living substance.'

(Genesis 7:23) The same thing occured with the generation of the Tower of Babel and the Sodomites. But in the
days of Moses, when I was defeated, I gained, because I
did not destroy Israel.' "

—Pesikta Rabbati 32:2

PART IV

G-D ANSWERS JOB

Introductory Note

A superficial reading of G-d's answer from the whirlwind could be misleading, for it appears irrelevant as a reply to Job. Job's reply to G-d proves otherwise. G-d begins by saying: "Who is it that darkens counsel by words without knowledge," and Job answers: "Truly I have spoken of what I did not understand."

Job's constant quest is for G-d to appear and meet him. Now his wish is granted. G-d speaks to him. G-d does not accuse Job of sin. G-d merely rebukes him by saying: "Who is it that darkens counsel by words without knowledge?" Job is vindicated as he had hoped, when G-d said to Eliphaz: "My anger is kindled against you and against your two friends; for you have not spoken of Me that which is right as has My servant Job."

Job, in his agony, questions Divine justice. G-d's answer depicts His justice and mercy to domestic animals and wild life. If G-d is just to animal life, He is just to man, even if man does not recognize it.

G-d's detailed description of creation and the natural laws is to remind Job that man was created to have dominion over nature and the world. Thus, if there is evil, it is man's task to conquer it.

159

Twice G-d speaks to Job. In response to G-d's description of creation, the mystery and marvels of the universe, Job replies: "I am insignificant, what can I answer You?"

To the second speech depicting G-d's providence, Job replies; "Truly I have spoken of what I did not understand, of things too wonderful for me, which I did not grasp . . . I have heard of You by the hearing of the ear, but now my eye sees You."

A fundamental principle in Judaism may be deduced from G-d's answer to Job. It is that life has a purpose. Beyond the description of G-d's power in creation and beyond the details of G-d's providence in the universe we detect an infinite purpose in nature, in life and the existence of mankind.

Chapters 38, 39 and 40:1-2

TEXT: CHAPTER 38

Then the Lord answered Job out of the whirlwind and said: Who is it that darkens counsel by words without knowledge? Gird up your loins like a man; I will question you and you may inform me. Where were you when I laid the foundations of the earth? Declare, if you have any understanding. Who fixed its measures, if you know who stretched a line over it? Upon what were its foundations embedded or who laid its corner stone? When the morning stars sang together and all the sons of G-d shouted for joy. Who enclosed the sea with doors when it burst forth, issuing from the womb; when I made the clouds its garment and dense darkness, its swaddling clothes. When I imposed upon it my decree setting for it bolts and doors. And I said: 'Thus far shall you come and no further, and here shall your proud waves be stayed.' Have you ever in your life commanded the morning? Or assigned its place to the dawn, that it take hold of the corners of the earth and the wicked be shaken out of it? It (the earth) changes like clay under the seal and they stand as a garment. Their light is withheld from the wicked and the arm of the proud is broken. Have you explored the sources of the sea or have

161

you walked in the recesses of the deep? Have the gates of death been revealed to you or have you seen the gates of the shadow of death? Have you comprehended the breadth of the earth? Declare if you know it all. Which is the way where light dwells and which is the place of darkness? That you may conduct it to its border and that you may perceive the path to its home. You know, for you were born then and the number of your days is great! Have you entered the storehouses of snow, have you seen the storehouses of the hail, which I have reserved for the time of trouble for the day of battle and war? Which is the way where light is distributed and the east wind spread itself over the earth? Who has divided a channel for the overflowing of water and a path for the thunderbolt to bring rain on no-man's land, the wilderness with no man in it; to satisfy waste and desolation and to cause the land of tender grass to sprout? Has the rain a father and who has begotten the dew drops? From whose womb came the ice and who gave birth to the frost of heaven? When water hardens like stone and the face of the deep is frozen. Can you bind the chains of pleiades or loose the cords of Orion? Can you bring out the constellations in the season and guide the Bear with its satellites? Do you know the laws of the heavens, can you establish its rule on the earth? Can you lift up your voice to the clouds that a flood of waters may cover you? Can you send lightnings that they may go and say to you, 'Here we are?' Who put wisdom in the inward parts? Or who has given understanding to the fowl? Who ordains the skies with wisdom, pours the waterskins of heaven? When dust hardens into a mass and the clouds stick firmly together? Do you hunt prey for the lioness and satisfy with sustenance the young lions? When they crouch in their dens and abide in the covert to lie in wait? Who provides the raven its food when its young ones cry to G-d and wander about without food?

TEXT: CHAPTER 39

Do you know the time when the mountain goats give birth; do you watch the travail of the hinds? Can you number the months they fulfill, and do you know the time they give birth? They crouch and deliver their offspring and cast off their young. Their young ones become strong; they grow up in the open field; they leave and do not return to them. Who has sent out the wild donkey, free, who loosened the bands of the swift donkey? Whose home I have made the wilderness and dwelling in the salt land. He scorns the noise of the city, the shouts of the driver he does not hear. The range of the mountains is his pasture and he searches after every green plant. Will the wild ox be willing to serve you? Or will he spend a night at your crib? Can you bind the wild ox with his rope in the furrow or will he harrow the valleys after you? Will you trust him because of his great strength, and leave him to do your work? Will you rely on him that he will return your seed and gather it to your threshing floor? The wing of the ostrich beats joyously but are her pinions and feathers like the kindly storks? For she leaves her eggs on the earth and lets them be warmed on the ground; and forgets that a foot may crush them and that the wild beast may trample them. She is hard on her young as though not her own; that her labor may be in vain gives her no concern. Because G-d had deprived her of wisdom, neither has he imparted to her understanding. At the time she flaps her wing on high she laughs at the horse and his rider. Have you given the horse his strength, have you clothed his neck with power? Have you made him leap like the locust, his majestic snorting strikes terror. They plunge, down into the valley rejoicing in strength; going on to meet the battle. He laughs at fear and is not terrified, he does not draw back from the sword. The arrow rattles about him, the flashing spear and javelin. With storms and rage he devours the ground and cannot believe that the trumpet is sounding. At the trumpet's blast he says 'Aha!' smelling the battle from afar, and the roar of the captains and shouting. Does the hawk fly by your wisdom and spread his wings toward the south? Is it at your command that the eagle mounts and makes his nest on high? On the cliff he dwells and lodges, upon the peak of the cliff and the stronghold.

From there he searches for food; his eyes see it from afar.
His young ones suck up blood and where the slain are,
there is he.

TEXT: CHAPTER 40:1-2
Then the Lord answered Job, saying: Will the reprover
strive with the Almighty? He who argues with G-d, let him
answer it.

COMMENTARY
Throughout the entire book, Job has one single yearn-
ing. "Even today is my complaint bitter; my affliction exceeds my groaning. Oh, that I knew where I might find
Him, that I might come to His judgment throne." (Job
23:2-4) His request and plea is now granted. This revelation of G-d is the answer. G-d's condemnation of Job's
three friends, Eliphaz, Bildad, and Zophar, again is a vindication of Job.

Job has complained that his personal suffering was un-
justified since he knows himself to be innocent of sin.
Then, in his misery, he accentuates the evil he sees around
him. All this would require an answer from G-d as to
justice and providence in the moral order of the world.

The answer from G-d in the whirlwind spells out Divine
wisdom in creation. Divine providence sustains order in
nature and provides sustenance to all living creatures.

The astronomical magnitude of the universe, recorded
in the Talmud, affects the problem under discussion.

The Talmud relates: "One might have thought that one
may inquire concerning the pre-creation period, therefore
the Bible teaches, 'Since the day that G-d created man upon
the earth.' One might have thought that one may not inquire concerning the six days of creation, therefore Scrip-
tures teaches 'The first days, which were before you.' One
might have thought one may inquire concerning what is
above and what is below, what before and what after,
therefore the text teaches, 'And from one end of heaven
unto the other.' What happens from one end of heaven

unto the other, you may inquire about, but you may not inquire what is above, what is below, what before, what after? (Talmud Chagiga 11b)

"There is still another heaven above the heads of the living creatures, for it is written: 'And over the heads of the living creatures there was a likeness of a firmament, like the color of the terrible ice, stretched forth over their heads above.' (Ezekiel 1:22) Thus far you have permission to speak, from there on you have no permission to speak, for it is written in the book of Ben Sira: 'Seek not things that are too hard for you and search not out things that are hidden from you. The things that have been permitted, think about them, but you have no business or need with the things that are secret.'

"What answer did the Heavenly voice give to the wicked one (Nebuchadnezzar) when he said, 'I will ascend above the heights of the clouds; I will be like the most High.' (Isaiah 14:14) A heavenly voice came forth and said to him, 'O wicked man, son of a wicked man, grandson of Nimrod, the wicked who stirred the whole world to rebellion against Me by his rule. How many are the years of a man? Seventy, but the distance from the earth to the firmament is a journey of five hundred years, and the thickness of the firmament is a journey of five hundred years, and likewise the distance between one firmament and the other.' " (Talmud Chagiga 13a)

From earth to the seventh heaven is a journey of 500 years (7 heavens and 7 interspatial distances), a total of 7000 years' journey.

The Talmud goes on to list angelic beings, the size of planets or stars ten times greater in size, equal to all distances listed before. Then instead of 7000 years journey it would become 70,000 years' journey.

These cosmic distances in space and time were calculated 2000 years ago. Modern astronomy is in agreement

165

with them in principle. For example, that the earth is 93 million miles away from the sun is an accepted fact. The sun is an ordinary star in our galaxy; the Milky Way consists of 100 billion stars. The nearest star outside our solar system is Alpha Centouri. A rocket ship travelling one million miles an hour would take 3000 years to reach it. The present observable universe is estimated to contain about ten billion galaxies.

The extremely complex universe proves how restricted and limited is man's grasp and comprehension about G-d's creation. How, then, can a mortal creature be a judge of G-d's ways?

Maimondes' comment will be helpful. "The origin of the error is to judge the whole universe by examining one single person. For an uninformed man believes that the whole universe exists for him; as if nothing else required consideration. If, therefore, anything happens to him contrary to his expectation, he at once concludes that the whole universe is evil. If he would take into consideration the whole universe, form an idea of it, and comprehend what a small part he is of the universe, he will find the truth." (Maimonides, *Guide for the Perplexed,* Volume 3 Chapter 12)

How then can Job's suffering be dealt with in isolation, as if he were the only one being in existence? A man's life can not be treated as if he were the only one in creation. The universe has a total purpose. Every man is only part of it. In his own eyes, Job stands alone. He sees himself as disconnected from the larger experience of the universe. His span of life and his grasp, limited by time and space, restricts his view, his understanding, and his judgments.

Job does not understand the visible order of the universe, how can he judge the invisible, the divine order of the universe?

G-d's speech teaches us that the universe and moral order cannot be judged from the vantage point of man, nor from the limited perspective of one human being. Suffering and evil is a reality in the cosmic world order.

G-d's silence on the subject of Job's suffering may also

imply that man is greatly responsible for the evil in the world. Man needs to accept a broader view. Man's view of evil does not call G-d's rule into question. Creation, nature, animate and inanimate matter, all undergo a struggle for existence. The author directs our view towards the outcome of the struggle as a proof of higher design.

Chapter 40

VERSES 3 THROUGH 5

TEXT:

Then Job answered the Lord and said: I am insignificant, what can I answer You? I lay my hand upon my mouth. I have spoken once and I will not reply, twice, but I will proceed no further.

COMMENTARY

Job is stunned by the divine declaration of the world order. Justice and mercy, is extended to animals and nature. This also silences his questions about himself. "I lay my hand upon my mouth." Job is relieved by G-d's answer. Job sees a design in the world even though he cannot fathom the mystery of his own life. (Suffering without apparent justice and guilt which goes unpunished.) His reasoning is obviously incapable of finding a solution to his quest. His reply would indicate that only humble faith in the Divine Will is a relief and a solution to the problem. Job accepts. He no longer asks. He will no longer speak because he realizes that life is a mystery beyond his comprehension. Job's second reply "Behold, I am insignificant, what can I answer you?" expresses his submission. Job, experiencing G-d's revelation and sensing the Divine Omnipotence over nature, submits himself to the hands of his Father in heaven.

The story is told about a blind child who is picked up and held by a visitor in his home. The father, testing the child, asks him, "Who is holding you, my son?" "I don't know," the child replied, "but you, my father, you know who is holding me."

Chapters 40:6-32 and 41

TEXT: CHAPTER 40:6-32

And the Lord answered Job out of the whirlwind and said: Gird up your loins like a man; I will question you and you may inform me.

Will you even annul my judgment? Will you make me guilty that you may be innocent? Have you an arm like G-d? And can you thunder with a voice like Him? Deck yourself now with majesty and grandeur and clothe yourself with glory and splendor. Scatter abroad your mighty wrath and as you see every one who is proud, humble him. Hide them in the dust together, bind their faces in the hidden place. Then I, too, will acknowledge to you that your own right hand can save you. Behold now the hippopotamus which I made along with you; he eats grass like an ox. Behold now his strength is in his loins and his power in the muscles in his belly. He can stiffen his tail like a cedar, and the sinews of his thighs are knit together. His bones are tubes of bronze; his limbs, like bars of iron. He is the first of the works of G-d; He that made him may bring his sword near him. For the mountains bring him his food and all beasts of the field play there. Beneath the lotus bushes he lies in the shadow of reeds and swamps. The lotus bushes cover him with their shadow, the willows of the brook surround him. Behold if a river flows violently he is not disturbed; he is confident though the Jordan surge up to his mouth. Can one seize Leviathan with a net or can you press down his tongue with a cord? Can you put a cord-line through his nose or pierce his jaw with a hook? Will he make many supplications or speak to you in soft words? Will he make a covenant with you that you may take him as a servant forever? Will you play with him as with a bird? Or will you put him on a leash for your maidens? Will traders bargain over him? Will they divide him amongst the merchants? Will you stick his skin with barbed irons, and his head with fishing spears? Lay your hand upon him; think of the struggle; you will not do it again.

TEXT: CHAPTER 41

Behold his hope (of subduing the monster) is disappointed; one is cast down even at the sight of him. No one is so fierce that he dare to stir him up; who then is able to stand before Me? Who has ever come before Me that I should repay him? Whatsoever is under the whole heaven is mine. I will not keep silent about his limbs and the account of his power and the grace of his structure. Who can strip off his outer garment? Who can penetrate his double armor? Who can open the doors of his face? Round about his teeth is terror, strong scales are his pride, shut up tight as with a seal. One is so near to the other that no air can enter between them. They are joined one to the other, they are interlocked so that they can not be separated. His sneezings flash forth light; his eyes are like the eyelids of the dawn. Out of his mouth go burning torches and sparks of fire leap forth. From his nostrils comes smoke as from a boiling pot and burning reeds. His breath kindles coal and a flame goes out of his mouth. Strength dwells in his neck, and before him leaps terror. The folds of his flesh are compact, firm upon him, immovable. His heart is firm like a rock, firm as the lower millstone.

When he raises himself up, the mighty are afraid;

because of panic they are beside themselves. If one strikes him with a sword it will not avail, not the spear, not the dart, nor the javelin. Iron he regards as straw and bronze as rotten wood. The arrow can not make him flee, for against him slingstones turn into stubble, and he laughs at the rattle of the javelin. His lower parts are like sharp potshards, he spreads out like a threshing sledge upon the mud. He makes the deep boil like a pot; he makes the sea like a pot of ointment. Behind him he leaves a shining path; one would think that the deep was hoary. Nowhere on earth is there one like him who was created to be without fear. He looks (down) upon all that is high, for he is king over all proud creatures.

COMMENTARY: CHAPTERS 40:6-32 and 41

Many readers of the Bible are puzzled by the tone of G-d's answer to Job. Job complains about evil and suffering in the world and G-d's answer begins by asking Job, "Where were you when I laid the foundation of the earth?" On the surface this may seem irrelevant.

How does this reply answer Job's questions? Let us consider this puzzling matter in reverse. Abraham is told by G-d that the corruption of Sodom is so great that He will destroy the city and annihilate its people. Abraham replies, "Far be it from you to do after this manner, to slay the righteous with the wicked, and that the righteous should be as the wicked, that be far from you. Shall not the judge of all the earth do justly?" Is that the way a mortal creature speaks to his immortal creator? This sounds more like a conversation between partners.

The example of Abraham can also be found with Moses: "And Moses returned unto the Lord and said 'Lord, wherefore have you brought evil on this people? Why is it that you have sent me? For since I came to Pharoah to speak in your name, he has dealt ill with this people; neither have you delivered your people at all." (Exodus 5:22-23) Also King David said: "G-d of retribution, Lord G-d of retribution appear. Rise up, O Judge of the earth, render to the arrogant what they deserve. How long shall the wicked exult?" (Psalms 94:1-3) Jeremiah pleaded: "You are righteous, O Lord, were I to contend with You. Yet will I reason with You, why does the way of the wicked prosper? Why do all the faithless live in comfort? You plant them and they take root. They grow and they bring forth fruit. Near are you in their mouths, but far from their thoughts." (Jeremiah 12:1-2) Habakuk asked: "Too pure of eyes are you to gaze upon faithless men and keep silent when the wicked swallows up a man more righteous than he." (Habakuk 1:13)

The prophet Isaiah said, "Come now let us reason together said the Lord." (Isaiah 1:18) The answer lies in the Jewish concept of the relationship between G-d and man.

This concept can be traced chronologically. The Torah tells us, "And G-d created man in His own image." (Genesis 1:27) Abraham Ibn Ezra explains that the word image "refers to the qualities of man's soul." Man was created with G-d like qualities, and, therefore, man has potential to perform G-d like acts. Then this brings responsibility, as it is followed by the charge, to man to "be fruitful and multiply and replenish the earth and subdue it." (Genesis 1:28)

Following the flood, a covenant was entered into between G-d and the whole of mankind. "As for me, behold, I establish My covenant with you and with your children after you." The rainbow is to become the symbol of the covenant. And G-d said: "This is the token of the covenant which I make between Me and you and every living creature that is with you for perpetual generations." (Genesis 9:9-12)

Then the second covenant was made between G-d and Abraham: "And I will establish my covenant between Me and you and your children after you, throughout their generations for an everlasting covenant, to be a G-d unto you and to your children after you. . . . This is my covenant which you should keep between Me and you and your children after you; every male among you shall be circumcised." (Genesis 17:7-10)

The above Biblical facts are embellished in Rabbinic literature. Rabbi Yochanan said, "Why was man created in the image of G-d? A parable: A king ruled over a city and built palaces there, provided it with all the necessities and all the people were subject to him. One day, he summoned all the people of the city and appointed over them one of his governors and said to them: Up to now, I concerned myself with all the requirements of the city and its buildings, towers and palaces. From now on, this governor shall be like me." (in my place)

"Similarly, (G-d said to man) 'I have put you in charge of all the world and all that is therein. As I ruled over it and constructed it according to My will, so shall you build and perform the work of the world. Therefore G-d made man in His image so that he should attend to all affairs of the world and its requirements as He did at first." (Zohar Hachodosh-Genesis 5)

"The existence of the world and the course of its development are in the hands of man, and depends on man's conforming to the character of his creator." (Maareches Hoelokis by Perez Barzelona)

The creation of the world and all its living creatures was culminated by the creation of man. Then the Torah tells, "No shrub of the field was yet on earth, and no herb of the field had yet sprung up, for the Lord G-d had not caused it to rain upon the earth and there was not a man to till the ground." (Genesis 2:5) This would teach us that after creation there was need for cooperation between G-d and man.

The Midrash Rabba, Genesis says: "Everything that was created during the six days of creation required completion. For example, the mustard seed is in need of sweetness and even man needs embellishment."

The responsibility of man's cooperation with G-d demanded more than his physical contribution. It also demanded his moral, ethical and creative contribution to the world.

The Talmud proclaims: "Every judge who performs justice in perfect truth is regarded as if he were a partner with the Holy One, blessed be He in the work of His creation." (Talmud Sabbath 10a)

G-d created the potential in man and in nature and it was man's task to develop them. On the one hand, one finds Divine creation and Providence and on the other hand, one finds human creativity and human production.

This partnership between G-d and man implied an imposed responsibility upon man.

The extent of this responsibility can best be seen in the development of medicine.

In the following, Malimonides insists that evil and sickness in the world are largely man made.

"The evils that befall man are of three kinds. Those caused by circumstances and ailments that may befall his physical being; second, those evils people cause each other; third, evils which everyone causes to himself by his own action. The numerous evils to which individual persons are exposed are due to the defects existing in the persons themselves. We complain and seek relief from our own faults; we suffer from the evils which we, by our own free will inflict on ourselves and ascribe them to G-d, who is far from being connected with them." (Maimonides, *Guide to the Perplexed,* Volume 3, Chapter 12)

In the case of Job's disease, his friends had a ready-made answer: G-d punished him for his sins. This categorical view, that the terrible diseases afflicting mankind are punishment for sin, is not necessarily true. Perhaps much of this is man's fault. If man's intellectual ingenuity and the economic means spent on wars, would have been used in research, we would, by now, have discovered cures for many of our fatal diseases. Suppose we knew today how to cure cancer as we know how to prevent polio. Would G-d suddenly have become more just? Does this not show that much physical illness and its suffering also rests with man. A Rabbinical inference regarding the creation of man will augment the above conclusion.

The question is asked, "How is it that following each process of creation there follows a divine refrain "And G-d saw that it was good." This follows the creation of the luminaries, vegetation, and animal life. However, following the creation of man the affirmation "It was good" is not mentioned. The answer given is that, whereas natural things were created perfect or complete, man was created incomplete, because it is man's task in life to perfect or complete himself.

The Bible teaches us that man was created in the image of G-d, with a potential to develop and complete himself. Man therefore has a purpose in the perfection of creation. Man is in a partnership with G-d to establish the Kingdom of Heaven on earth.

An illustration from "The Beginning":

The first sentence in the Bible reads "In the beginning G-d created the heaven and the earth." We sense here a dualistic creation, heaven above and earth below. The Rabbis accentuate the difference and separate aspects of heaven and earth. These are two worlds.

On the one hand there is heaven that the Psalmist speak of as "The heaven is G-d's heaven." (Psalms 115: 16) This is a spiritual world. Nowhere is there an indication or goal to add or detract, to repair or impair heaven. This is a perfect and complete creation. It is G-d's habitation.

On the other hand, the Psalmist speaks of "The earth He has given to mankind." The earth was not a complete and perfect creation as was the heaven. The earth was destined to be corrected and to be completed. Adam was charged "to cultivate and guard it."

At the conclusion of the story of creation we meet again with the specific differences between heaven and earth. "And the heavens and the earth were finished." There follows: "And on the seventh day G-d finished His work which He had made." This may well refer to the first item mentioned—the heaven. The concluding phrase of that sentence says, "And He rested on the seventh day." This would then refer to the earth. There is a distinct difference between the work that was "finished," the heaven, and G-d's merely "resting" after the incomplete creation of fashioning the earth.

The paragraph concludes by repeating the concept of resting. "Because on it He rested from all His work which G-d created and made." The last word "and made" using the past tense is literally incorrect translation. It should be translated "which G-d created to make." To translate it with a future tense supports our view that the earth is still unfinished. "It is man's glorious privilege to help finish it. He can, by his life, hasten the triumph of the forces of good in the universe." (Rabbi J. H. Hertz)

This then is the very key to the Book of Job. G-d created the world. His power is manifest in nature, in natural laws. The Bible (as has been shown in this commentary) indicates that a mandate was given to man to develop himself and to gain control over nature.

G-d's speech from the whirlwind addresses itself to that view. In this speech you find a poetic resume of creation and of continued Providence in nature, vegetation and living creatures.

It is man's task to become a partner in creation by developing his potential, to avoid evil, and eliminate suffering. G-d's revelation and the speech of His part in creation implies man's failure in not fulfilling his share, "to cultivate and guard" life on earth.

Job responds that he "retracts his words and repents." This can reflect his realization that man has not lived up to his part of this partnership to make this a better world.

Chapter 42
VERSES 1 THROUGH 6

TEXT

Then Job answered the Lord and said: I know that you can do all things and that no plan of yours can be restrained. Who is he who hides counsel without knowledge? Truly I have spoken of what I did not understand, of things too wonderful for me which I did not grasp. Hear now and I will speak, I will ask of You and You will inform me. I have heard of You by the hearing of the ear but now my eye sees You. Therefore I retract (my words) and repent for I am dust and ashes.

COMMENTARY

Job senses in G-d's speech man's weakness, the limits of his comprehension of the natural world, his lack of knowledge of G-d's Providence. The universal dimensions of G-d's declarations evoke Job's reply. "I know that You can do all things and no plan of Yours can be restrained."

Job now admits. "Truly I have spoken of what I did not understand of things too wonderful for me, which I did not grasp."

Job has now been transformed. He feels vindicated by

G-d's revelation. He concludes: "I had heard of You by the hearing of the ear, but now my eye sees You." He was seeking a reason for his personal suffering, but he found something more important in G-d's answer to him. Job has now found the wisdom of higher standards of justice; that it is impossible for a mortal creature to comprehend or judge the Divine order of the world. He found total faith.

The following story is a fitting parable of Job's experience. A wealthy man, fearful that he may be robbed in time of war, hid his valuables in secret places in his house.

The man died suddenly and his son did not know these hidden places. One day he was counting his last few silver coins. One coin dropped to the floor and rolled away before he could reach it.

Since he had little money, he desperately searched for his lost coin. As he tore out the floor boards, under the planks, he discovered a chest full of gold. This impelled him to look further. He never found the lost silver coin, but he found new treasures.

Parables and Anecdotes

TO KNOW G-D

"Abraham perceived G-d, by himself and nobody taught him this knowledge. He is one of four human beings who accomplished this. Job perceived G-d, by himself as it is said: 'More than what I apportioned for myself have I treasured the words of His mouth." (Job 23:12)

Hezekiah, king of Judah, likewise perceived G-d by himself, since it is written concerning him: "'Butter and honey shall be eat, when he knows how to refuse the evil and choose the good.' (Isaiah 7:15) The King Messiah, also perceived G-d by himself."

—Midrash Rabba Numbers 14:2

179

"Show me your ways O Lord" (Psalms 25:4). Rabbi Berachia said in the name of Rabbi Yochanan: 'This can be likened to a physician who had a disciple and taught him all the cures except the cure of one certain disease. He said to him: 'You have revealed to me all the cures in the world except the cure of that affliction. I beg you, reveal it to me.'

So Moses said to G-d: 'Show me your ways.' (Exodus 33:13) and G-d made it known to him as it is said: 'He made known His ways unto Moses.' (Psalms 103:7). 'Show me, I pray You, Your glory.' (Exodus 33:18) Show me that quality with which you conduct the world. He said to him: 'You cannot fathom my qualities.' "

—Midrash T'hilim 25:4

"Parable of a man who had fallen into the sea: The captain of the boat threw him a rope and said: 'Cling to this rope and do not let go of it, if you loosen your hold upon it you will drown.' Similarly the Holy One blessed be He said to Israel: 'So long as you cleave to the commandments you cleave unto the Lord your G-d and are alive everyone of you this day.' (Deuteronomy 4:4)

And as it is said, 'Take fast hold of instruction, let her not go; keep her, for she is your life.' "

—Midrash Rabba Numbers 17:7

"Job said: 'The stranger did not lodge in the street.' (Job 31:32) There is no creature that G-d rejects, but He accepts them all. The gates are open at every hour and all who wish to enter may enter. The above sentence concludes: 'My doors I opened to roadside' meaning that G-d tolerates His creatures."

—Midrash Rabba Exodus19:4

"Rabbi Huna said: 'Whatever things you see are but a fragment of G-d's ways as it says: 'Behold those are but the outer edges of His ways; only a whisper of Him do we catch; who can perceive the thunder of His omnipotence.' (Job 26:14) Rabbi Huna said: 'When thunder comes out in its full force no creature can understand it. It is not written, none perceive but 'Who can perceive.'

The intelligent man knows His hints and His thoughts (to lead him to repentance).

Rabbi Huna said: 'If you cannot comprehend the essential nature of thunder, can you comprehend the essence of the world?'

Rabbi Nachman said: 'This may be compared to a thicket of reeds which no man could enter, for whoever entered lost his way. What did a certain clever man do? He cut down some reeds and entered, then cut down more and penetrated further. Thus he entered through the clearing and went out. Then all began to enter through his clearing.

Rabbi Nachman gave another illustration. 'Imagine a large palace with many doors, so that whoever entered, lost his way. What did a certain wise man do? He took a ball of cord and tied it near the door then all began to enter and go out by the means of this clue.'

Rabbi Shimon ben Yochoee said: "This may be compared to a mortal king who built a palace. People entered it and criticized. If the columns were taller it would be beautiful; if the walls were higher it would be beautiful; if the ceiling were higher it would be beautiful. But will any man say 'Oh, that I had three eyes or three feet?' Surely not.' "—Midrash Rabba Genesis 12

"Rabbi Chomo ben Chanina began: 'Do you know this as from old times since man was placed on earth' (Job 20:4) This may be compared to a country which received its supplies from donkey drivers who used to ask each other, what was the market price today? Those who supplied goods on the sixth day would ask of those who supplied on the fifth day; the fifth of its fourth day; the fourth of its third day; the third of the second; the second of the first; but of whom was the first day supplier to ask? Surely of the citizens who were engaged in the public affairs of the country. Thus G-d's creation of each day asked one another 'Which creatures did G-d create among you today? The 6th asked of the 5th; the 5th of the 4th; the 4th of the 3rd; the 3rd of the 2nd, and the second of the 1st, of whom has the 1st to ask? Surely, of the Torah, which preceded the creation of the world by 2000 years, as it is written 'Then I was with Him as an architect.' (Proverbs 8:30) That is the meaning of 'Do you know this as from old time?' The Torah knows what was before the creation of the world, but you have no business to inquire about it except what has been 'Since man was placed upon earth.'

Rabbi Elozer said in Bar Sira's name: That which is too great for you do not inquire, what is too hard for you do not investigate, that which is too wonderful for you, you don't know; what is hidden from you do not ask. Study what was permitted you, you have no business with hidden things.

—Midrash Rabba Genesis 8:2

"Our great teacher Rabbi Judah Hanassi said: 'We are indebted to Job, because he added to everything that Elihu said. Job said to his friends: 'Do you imagine that even all you have said exhausts all His praise? Who can declare all those praises and mighty deeds of the Lord? All the things you have said. Why, 'These are but the outer edges of His ways' (Job 26:14).

Elihu said: 'The Almighty, whom we cannot find out.' (Job 37:23) He who hears this verse may exclaim: 'Perhaps this, Heaven forbid, is blasphemy.' But this is what Elihu meant: We will never find G-d's strength fully displayed toward any of His creatures with burdensome laws, but comes to each one according to his strength. For know you that if G-d had come upon Israel with the full might of his strength when He gave them the Torah, they would not have been able to withstand it, as it says, 'If we hear the voice of the Lord our G-d any more, than we shall die.' (Deuteronomy 5:22)

G-d, however, came upon them according to their individual strength, for it says 'The voice of the Lord is with power' (Psalms 29:4). It does not say "with His power' but 'with power,' that is according to the power of each individual.' "

—Midrash Rabba Truma 34

"At that time He showed Moses all the treasures that are the reward of the righteous for their respective deeds. Moses asked: Whose treasure is this? He answered: The Masters of the Torah. (Moses asked) And whose treasure is this? And G-d replied: For those who honor them. Then He showed Moses a treasure greater than all the rest.

Moses said: Master of the Universe, whose is this great treasure? He said to him: He who has none of his own, freely I give him from this, as it is said: 'And I will be gracious to whom I will be gracious and I will show mercy to whom I shall show mercy.' " (Exodus 33:19)

—Midrash Tanchuma Exodus Ki Sissa

"Antignus of Socho received the tradition from Shimon the Just. He used to say: 'Be not like the servants who serve the master for the sake of receiving a reward, but be like servants who serve the master without the expectation of receiving a reward; and let the fear of heaven be upon you.' "

—Avoth 1:3

TO FIND G-D

"How does a man find his Father who is in Heaven? He finds him by kind deeds (to man) and study of Torah (to G-d). And G-d finds man through love, brotherhood, and respect; through companionship, truth and peace; through learning and less business; through service of the teachers

183

and discussion of the disciples; through a good heart and decent behavior; through 'no' that is really 'no' and 'yes' that is really 'yes.' "

—Seder Eliyahu Rabba 23

"For two and a half years a debate went on between the School of Shammai and the School of Hillel. The School of Shammai said that it were better for man not to have been created than to have been created. And the School of Hillel maintained that it is better for man to have been created than not to have been created. They finally took a vote and decided that it was better for man not to have been created than to have been created, but now that he has been created, let him search his past deeds, or as others report, let him examine his future actions.

—Eruvin 13b

MAN REBELS

"Rabba taught: 'What is meant by the verse (Job 12:5) 'In the thought of one who is at ease, there is contempt for misfortune, ready for those whose foot slips.' This teaches that when Noah rebuked them (the generation of the flood) and spoke to them words that were as hard as fiery flints, they derided him. They said to him 'Old man, what is this ark for?' He replied, 'G-d will bring a flood upon you.' 'A flood of what?' They jeered.

"If a flood of fire we have 'Alitha' (a fire extinguishing demon). Should He bring a flood of water? If He brings it up from the earth we have iron plates with which we can cover the earth (to prevent the water from coming up). If from heaven we have something called 'Akob' (to protect the head against rain).' "

—Sanhedrin 108b

"Parable: It may be likened to a man who had a lean cow but of a large build. He fed it on horse beans and it kicked him. The man said to the creature, 'What caused

184

you to kick me but the horse beans on which I fed you.' Rabbi Acha said, that is what the proverb declares. 'He whose stomach is full increases deeds of evil.' "

"It is like a company of men on board a ship. One of them took a drilling tool and began to bore a hole under him. The other passengers told him, 'What are you doing?' He replied: 'What has that to do with you? Am I not making the hole under my seat?' They answered: 'But the water will enter and drown us all.' "

—Midrash Rabba Leviticus 4:6

"And every living substance was destroyed which was upon the face of the earth." (During the flood, Genesis 7:23) If man sinned, how did the beasts sin? A Sage taught on the authority of Rabbi Joshua ben Korcha: 'This may be compared to a man who made a wedding for his son and prepared a banquet with every variety of food. Subsequently his son died, then he arose and broke up the feast. He said: 'Have I not prepared all this for my son? Now that he is dead, what need have I of the banquet?' Thus, too, G-d said: 'Did I not create the animals and the beasts for the sake of man? Now that man has sinned, what need have I of the animals and the beasts?' "

—Sanhedrin 108a

Rabbi Joseph taught: "What is the meaning of the verse, 'And none of you shall go out at the door of his house until the morning? (Exodus 12:22) Once permission has been granted to the destroyer, he does not distinguish between the righteous and wicked. What is more, he even begins with the righteous first!' Rabbi Joseph wept at this, saying: 'So much are they (the righteous) considered as nothing!' Abaye said to him: 'This is for their advantage.' (That the righteous may not see the coming evil.)

Baba Kamma 60a

MAN ACTS

"In the hour when G-d created the first man, he took him past all the trees of the Garden of Eden. He then said to him: 'See my works, how beautiful and excellent they are. All I have created, I created for you. Think upon this and do not damage and destroy my world, for if you damage it, there is no one to set it right after you."

—Midrash Rabba Ecclesiastes 8:28

Rabbi Shimon ben Gamaliel said: "The world is sustained by three principles: Truth, Justice, and Peace, as it is said 'You shall execute Truth, Justice, and Peace within your gates.' " (Zechariah 8:16)

—Avoth 1:18

King David said: "I, what am I in the world? I have been fearful in the midst of my joy, and I have rejoiced in the midst of my fear, but my love has surpassed them both."

—Seder Elyohu Rabba 3

PART V
EPILOGUE

Introductory Note

The epilogue recaptures the mood and language of the prologue. G-d rebukes the friends of Job and will forgive them only if Job intercedes on their behalf. When Job does so, G-d accepts Job's plea.

Job's family and many friends return to him. They bring gifts and comfort to him now that he does not need their sympathy.

The book has a happy ending. G-d restores in double measure all that Job had lost.

Chapter 42
VERSES 7 THROUGH 9

TEXT

And it was after the Lord had spoken these words to Job, the Lord said to Eliphaz, the Tamanite, My anger is kindled against you and against your two friends, for you have not spoken of Me that which is right as has My servant Job. Now, then take seven bulls and seven rams and go to My servant Job and offer them as a burnt offering for yourselves; and My servant Job shall pray for you, for only him will I accept; not to deal harshly with you for you have not spoken of Me that which is right as has My servant Job.

So Eliphaz the Tamanite, Bildad the Shuhite and Zophar the Naamathite went and did as the Lord told them and the Lord accepted Job's plea.

COMMENTARY

In the epilogue, G-d addresses Eliphaz, "My anger is kindled against you and against your two friends because you have not spoken of Me the thing that is right, as has My servant Job." G-d rebukes the three friends of Job "for not having spoken of Me that which is right." The reader sees the obvious truth in this criticism. The friends were wrong in insisting that Job's suffering was punishment for his sins. They were wrong in advancing an earthly theology that it pays to be good and to serve G-d for the sake of receiving a reward. They were dogmatic that suffering comes from sin. They were censured for wrong thinking and bad judgment.

The following story is very applicable to Job's friends.

A grandson asks his grandfather; "People say you are a very wise man. Tell me, how did you become so wise?" The grand-father is pleased with his compliment and answers. "I have become wise, I suppose, from using good judgment."

"But grand-father how did you get good judgment?" The grand-father thinks a moment and replies, "One gets good judgment from experience." The grand-son is further inquiring "How did you get experience?" He answered, "experience you get from bad judgment."

Chapter 42

VERSES 10 THROUGH 17

TEXT

Then the Lord restored the fortunes of Job, when he interceded for his friends, and the Lord doubled all of Job's possessions. Then came to him all his brothers and all his sisters and all his former friends and they ate food with him in his house and they consoled him and comforted him for all the misfortunes that the Lord had brought him; each man gave him a piece of money and a golden ring. .

So the Lord blessed the end of Job more than his beginning; he had fourteen thousand sheep and six thousand camels and a thousand yoke of oxen and thousand female donkeys. He had fourteen sons and three daughters. And he called the name of the first Jemima and the name of the second Keziah, and the name of the third Keren Hapuch.

In all the land there were not found women as fair as the daughters of Job; and their father gave them an inheritance among their brothers. After this Job lived one hundred and forty years, and he saw his sons and grandsons, four generations. So Job died old and satisfied with days (life).

COMMENTARY:

The restoration of Job to his position of health and wealth is viewed by the rabbis as his facing a new world and a new life. In addition to facing a new world, he was also confronted with the challenge which a new life presents.

There were five men in the Bible who faced a new world. Noah, who lived ten generations after Adam, was the only righteous man in a corrupt world. In the Biblical book Genesis we are told "and the earth was corrupt before G-d, for all flesh had corrupted his way upon the earth. For the earth is filled with violence and I will destroy them." A flood lasting 40 days wiped out all life except that of Noah and his family. Specimens of all living creatures were also saved in Noah's ark.

Noah, then saw a world destroyed by a flood and, then, experienced a world born anew.

Joseph, beloved son of Jacob, was disliked by his brothers. This happened during the early, formative history of our people. The book of Genesis relates that Joseph's dreams of superiority over his brothers caused them to hate him. Once Joseph came to meet them in the fields of pasture. There the brothers conspired to kill him, but finally decided to sell him into slavery, to a band of Egyptians.

Joseph suffered a world of torture and imprisonment, but later became viceroy to the King of Egypt with power and honor.

Moses: About 3500 years ago the Jewish people were slaves in Egypt. One of the evil decrees against them was that all male children be eliminated at birth. At this time Moses was born.

He was hidden for three months. Miraculously he was saved from the waters of the Nile by an Egyptian Princess and raised in the royal palace. Later, he discovered that he is one of the enslaved Israelites. Moses watched his people enslaved in a world of cruel bondage but later he led them to freedom, liberty and G-d's revelation on Mount Sinai. Moses, too, had to face a new world and new challenges.

Mordechai, the hero of the story of Purim lived in Persia in the fourth century B.C.E. The Book of Esther relates how a weak King accepted the barbaric proposal of the wicked Haman to exterminate all the Jews in the Kingdom. The new queen, Esther, niece of Mordechai pleads with the King for the lives of her people. They are saved.

Mordechai lived through a world in which he and his people were threatened with total annihilation. He then faced a new world where those who wanted to hang him were themselves hanged and his people achieved happiness and peace.

Job went through a life of trial, dreadful disease, physical and spiritual suffering. He lived to gain recovery and restoration.

He regained a complete faith in a new world of peace and tranquility.

An analysis of how these five men met the challenges of their new lives bring to us a message important to the understanding of the Book of Job.

Historically we know that all but one met their challenges to go on to a greater destiny.

Joseph facing a new world of honor and power tells his famine stricken brothers; "G-d did send me before you to preserve life" and uses his position to help his family and the people of Egypt. Moses chosen to lead the Israelites to freedom from physical slavery brings them to Mt. Sinai to receive the ten commandments and accept the Torah. Mordechai not only saved his people from total annihilation, but brought them to a rededication of their heritage. Job has now risen to such heights of spiritual understanding that G-d declares "and my servant Job shall pray for you for only to him will I show favor . . . and the Lord accepted Job's plea." Job, instead of carrying a grudge against his friends who tormented him, prayed for them.

Noah alone failed to realize that a new world meant new responsibilities, new opportunities and new duties. The Bible relates; "and Noah, the man of earth began and planted a vineyard. And he drank of the wine and became intoxicated and lay uncovered in his tent." The commentators interpret "began" "voyachal" Noah made himself base "chol," because he should have planted something other

194

than a vineyard. The Midrash adds that "man of earth" means that he set his face to the earth and to earthly things alone.

In a time of great opportunity he became drunk and it led him to deterioration and failure.

There seems to be one obvious contrast between the life experience of Noah who failed and the four who succeeded and rose to spiritual heights.

Joseph was persecuted by his brothers, was placed in a pit and was sold into slavery and imprisoned in Egypt! Moses fled for his life from Egypt and was reduced from princely state in a royal palace to that of a shepherd in a tent. Mordechai lived in the shadow of the gallows intended for him. Job suffered miserably as is described in this book. Noah alone faced a new world without any previous sorrow or suffering.

It is fair to speculate that the suffering of Joseph, Moses, Mordechai and Job was a preparation for understanding of their fellow man. If so, we may detect a purpose in their suffering. It expanded their lives. It extended their vision and it expressed itself greatly in compassion for their fellow man.

Parables and Anecdotes

PRAYER:
"Rovo said to Rabbi ben Mori, "From where is derived the lesson taught by our Rabbis that one prays for mercy for his fellow while he himself is in need of the same thing, he will be answered first? He replied: "As it is written 'And the Lord changed the fortune of Job when he prayed for his friends.' (Job 42:10)
—Baba Kamma 92a

BOOK OF JOB:
"Rabbi Yochanan on reading the book of Job used to say: 'The end of a man is to die and the end of cattle is to

195

be slaughtered and all are doomed to die. Happy is he who has been reared in Torah and whose labor was in Torah; Who pleased his creator and has grown up with a good name. Just of such a good man Solomon said: 'A good name is better than good oil." (Proverbs 7:1)

—Brochoth 17a